Herny William Clarke

History of Tithes from Abraham to Queen Victoria

Herny William Clarke
History of Tithes from Abraham to Queen Victoria
ISBN/EAN: 9783337323219
Printed in Europe, USA, Canada, Australia, Japan
Cover: Foto ©ninafisch / pixelio.de

More available books at **www.hansebooks.com**

THE HISTORY OF TITHES

FROM

ABRAHAM TO QUEEN VICTORIA

BY

HENRY W. CLARKE.

LONDON
GEORGE REDWAY
YORK STREET, COVENT GARDEN
MDCCCLXXXVII

CONTENTS.

	PAGES
INTRODUCTION,	11-27

CHAPTER I.

THE HISTORY OF TITHES BEFORE THE CHRISTIAN ERA,   1-4

Abraham the first recorded payer of tithes, 1. Jacob's ladder, 1. Old Testament directions for the payment of tithes, 1-2. When tithes ceased among the Jews, 3. The heathen nations paid tithes, 3. The foolish story of Adam having paid tithes, 3, 4.

CHAPTER II.

FROM THE CHRISTIAN ERA TO A.D. 400,   5-13

The maintenance of the ministers in Apostolic times, 1, 2. The "Apostolical Constitutions" said to be collected by Clement I., 6, 7. Anglican divines supporting the claim to tithes on these Constitutions, 7, 8. The division of the offerings and oblations, 8. Constantine's edict, 8. Are Christians justified in adopting the Mosaic law for the payment of tithes? 9. Tithes given at first as spontaneous offerings, 10. "The Englishman's Brief on behalf of his National Church," 10, 11; the effect of this mixture of fiction and facts, 11-13.

CHAPTER III.

FROM A.D. 400 TO A.D. 787,   14-30

The earliest supposed council which ordained the payment of tithes, 14. Dr J. S. Brewer's mistakes, 14, 15. "To live of the Gospel" does not refer to the payment of tithes, 15. Passages of Scripture distorted to prove the early origin of tithes, 16. Britain as a "buffer" to Ireland, 16. Augustin's mission to England, 17, 18. Episcopi clerus and mater ecclesia, 18, 19. Duties of the itinerant preachers, 19. The

Contents.

PAGES

origin of parish churches and their endowments, 20, 21. Edgar's laws in increasing parish churches, 22. Origin of lay patronage, 22-24. Augustin's first question to Pope Gregory, 24, 25. Bishops separating themselves from their clergy, 25. Bishops giving up their shares of tithes; parochial clergy adopting tripartite division, 26. Reasons for tripartite division of tithes in England, 27-29. Popes' influence in Church of England, commencing with Augustin's mission, 29, 30.

CHAPTER IV.

FROM A.D. 787 TO A.D. 1000, ... 31-46

Charlemagne's first public lay law for payment of tithes, 31. Milman's remarks on such law, 31, 32. Hallam's remarks, 32, 33. First legates to England from the pope, 33. The influence of the Roman Church in England, 33, 34, 38. King Offa's murder and grant of tithes, 34. King Ethelwulph's charter granting tithes, 35-39. Ingulph's construction of this charter, 37. Confirmations of tithes, 39. Definition of various tithes, 40-43. "Modus decimandi," 43. Edgar's laws, 44, 45. Mother churches should give decent maintenance to daughter churches, 45, 46.

CHAPTER V.

FROM A.D. 1000 TO A.D. 1215, ... 47-62

Impetus to the building of monasteries, 47. The monks initiated the practice of appropriating tithes to monasteries, 48. Chapters, nuns, and others followed their example, 48. The lay patrons arbitrarily appropriated tithes and churches to whom they wished, 48, 49. Third Council of Lateran, 1180, condemned arbitrary appropriations, 49. Its decrees opposed by English lay owners, 50. A national assembly at Westminster, 1125, condemned lay appropriations, 50. Gradually ceased in the reigns of Rich. I. and John, 51. Fourth Lateran Council, 1215, gave parsons the parochial right to tithes, 51. The effect of the decrees of this Council, 52. Tithes appropriated to monasteries were of two kinds, 54, 55. 15 Rich. II. c. 6 orders competent sum to be distributed among the poor out of wealth of Church, 55. Parish priests kept all the tithes to themselves. 55. Vicars perpetual created by 4 Henry IV., c. 12, 56. This "vicar perpetual" not to be confounded wih the "perpetual curate," 57. Abuse of parochial freehold tenure; the parochial autocrat; how the abuse may be remedied, 58, 59. Number of parishes in England and Wales at the Reformation, 59; numbers in 1831 and 1887; number of clergy in 1887, 60. Provincial synods ordering the payment of tithes, 61. Domesday book, 61, 62.

CHAPTER VI.

FROM A.D. 1215 TO THE DISSOLUTION OF MONASTERIES, 61-79

Most important English canon of 1295, for payment of tithes, 61-64. Canon of 1344 led to bitter strife, 65-67. First victory of the young House of Commons as regards tithes, 66. Statute of Mortmain, 67. Action of House of Commons against canons for payment of tithes without assent of Commons, 68. Some views in the "Brief" combated, 68-75. Dr Howley of Canterbury and Dr Sumner of Winchester at loggerheads in the "Lords," 76. "Jus parochiale" and "jus Commune," 77, 78. Extra parochial lands, 78, 79.

CHAPTER VII.

MONASTERIES, ... 80-96

A sketch of the origin and progress of monasteries in England. 80. The Danes destroyed the monasteries, 82. King Edgar rebuilt them, 83. His leading church ideas, 84. The English monks passed through three reformations. The influence of the Norman Conquest on monasteries, 86-89. Monasteries built from William I. to Henry VI., 89. The religious revolutionary wave which passed over England in thirteenth century. 90. The preaching of the Dominicans, Franciscans, and John Wickliffe, 90-93. Earl of Chester's charter to the monastery of Chester, 94-95.

CHAPTER VIII.

INFEUDATIONS—EXEMPTION FROM PAYING TITHES, . 97-100

The Third Lateran Council and infeudations, 97. The infeudations of Henry VIII. and his son, 97-98. Exemption from paying tithes by religious houses, 98-100.

viii *Contents.*

CHAPTER IX.

THE DISSOLUTION OF MONASTERIES, ... 101-111
    PAGES

Eight precedents Henry VIII. had to guide him in dissolving monasteries, 101-103. Collegiate endowments from monastic properties, 103-104. Henry VIII.'s action in dissolving monasteries, 104-110. Laws passed for the payment of tithes, 110-111.

CHAPTER X.

THE COMMUTATION ACT OF 1836, 6 AND 7 WILL. IV., C. 71, 112-139

Tithes a tax on industry, 112. Paley's and Adam Smith's views of tithes, 112-113. Lord Althorp's attempts and failures, 113-114. Peel's, 114. Lord Russell's Commutation Bill, 114-116. The Act illustrated, 116-117. The 80th section out of which landlords contracted themselves, 117-118. Embarrassments brought about by such contracts, 118-120, Dual landlordism, 121. The great injustice of tithe rent charges, 121, 122. Have the clergy at the present time lost two millions sterling by the Commutation Act? 123, 124. Proposed redemption of tithes, 124, 125. Extraordinary tithe rent charge, 125-127. Duty on hops repealed, 128. Market Gardens Act, 1873; Orchards, 128, 129. Extraordinary Tithe Redemption Act, 129-131. Table showing the septennial average prices of the three corns from 1835 to 1885, tithe rent charges for fifty years, 133. Tithe rent charge in Wales, 134. State of the Church in Wales, 135-137. Retrospective view of tithes in England, 137-139.

CHAPTER XI.

TITHES IN THE CITY AND LIBERTIES OF LONDON, . 140-150

How the London citizens, in early times, supported their clergy and churches, 140. Bishop Roger's Constitution, 141. Archbishop Arundell's additional eleven penny tax, 142. Henry VIII.'s laws for payment of tithes in London, 143, 144. Charles II.'s law on London tithes after the great fire, 145, 146. St Bartholomew's Hospital, London, 146, 147. Parishes not destroyed by the fire to pay 2s. 9d. in the pound, 147. Christ Church Tithe Act, 147, 148. City of London Tithe Act, 148. St Botolph-Without, Aldgate, Mr Esdaile, lay impropriator, 148-150.

Contents.

CHAPTER XII.

REDEMPTION OF TITHE RENT CHARGE, . . . 151-164

Tithe Commissioners' Report, 151. Clerical appropriators, 152. Net revenue of tithe rent charge in 1886, 152. Amounts of redemption and incomes for 20 and 25 years' purchase, 153, 154. Tithe rent charge for 1887. Gross and net revenues in 1887, 155. Capital and incomes in 1887 from 20 and 25 years' purchase, 156. Redemption viewed from another point, 157-159. Lay impropriators, schools, colleges, &c., 159-161. Remarks on the revenues of clerical appropriators and parochial incumbents, 162, 163. Landlords and redemption [125, Chapter X.], 163, 164. Observations on the redemption scheme, 160-164.

CHAPTER XIII.

SOME REMARKS ON "A DEFENCE OF THE CHURCH OF ENGLAND AGAINST DISESTABLISHMENT," BY THE EARL OF SELBORNE. NEW EDITION, 1877, . 165-176

The Earl ignores the grants of tithes by Kings Offa and Ethelwulph, 165-167. He denies that the tithes were divided in England, 168. He is the special pleader and ex parte writer for the Church, 168, 169. His inconsistency and partiality, 169-171. His statements answered, 166-174. Repairs of churches by parishioners, their origin, 172-176.

INTRODUCTION.

WHEN engaged in writing the History of the Rise, Progress, and Present Position of the Ecclesiastical Commission for England, I had to deal with the endowments of the Church. Those derived from tithes were the most important. My desire was to collect facts as to their origin in the Christian Church generally, and in the Church of England particularly. In searching after truth and facts, I experienced no little difficulty in arriving at correct conclusions, from the various contradictory statements on the subject. One party saw in the payment of tithes a continuity of old Scriptural laws in the Christian Church, and which Christians were bound to pay, whether they liked it or not; passages from the Old and New Testaments were distorted, and forced meanings given to them; apostolical constitutions were forged in support of the payment of the tithe tax. What Isidore did as regards his forged decretals we find other early writers did as regards tithes, and sham miracles are paraded in their works in support of tithes in the Christian Church. Another party, whose views John Selden is the impartial exponent, took a more correct view of the subject, and denied that the patriarchal custom, or Mosaic law, bound Christians to the payment of tithes *quâ* tithes. They asserted with truth that the Divine Founder of the Christian religion and His Apostles left behind them no written instructions for the payment of tithes, but the latter did state how the ministers were to be maintained—viz., on the purely voluntary principle. I am certain, it is against the whole tenour of the New Testament writings, that any funds for the support of those who minister at the altar, or in building or repairing sanctuaries for divine worship, should be collected *vi et armis*. It is revolting to all Christian principles enunciated in the New Testament that men should be imprisoned, or their goods seized, or, even as it happened in Ireland within this century, be shot dead, because they refused to pay tithes. But there have been, and there are still, men in England who unblushingly justify all the above means by which an odious and unscriptural tax should be collected for the support of the ministers of the Church of England. On the other hand, there have been, and there are still, in England noble-minded,

Introduction.

sympathetic, and large-hearted Christi
have conscientiously opposed such taxa
unscriptural.

For centuries, after the Christian Era, Christians paid no tithes *quâ* tithes. In some the Episcopal writings of the second and thi. centuries, suggestions are thrown out, but nothing more, recommending the payment of tithes according to the Mosaic law, certainly not with the view of handing over to the ministers all the proceeds of such payments, but to supplement the Church funds for the support of the poor, the fabric of the churches, and the ministers. According to the Mosaic law, the priests received but the one-hundredth part of the tithes, for the Levites had also to be provided for.

It was not until the fifth century that canons were passed for the payment of tithes. They were unknown in the British Church when Augustin landed on our shores, at the end of the sixth century. His mission was a mixture of good and evil. It was good, because it introduced among the Anglo-Saxons an active evangelical spirit. It was evil, because it formed the first link of an alliance between the Church of England and the Church of Rome. From that time forward the bishops of Rome interfered in the discipline and

Introduction.

of the English Church. They sent their
to England to attend provincial synods,
pass canons for the payment of tithes,
ut consulting the laity. The Church of
ie never allows the laity to have a share or a
ice in any ecclesiastical matters. That was
always, and is still, the most prominent feature in
her organisation. In the eighth century, tithe free-
will offerings were first given in England by a few
individuals. In the ninth century Charlemagne
passed the first lay law for the payment of tithes
in his dominions. This was a great victory gained
by the Church. His father, in A.D. 755, gave
Ravenna to Pope Stephen III., and thus initiated
the temporal territorial power of the popes. Milman in his history gives a sad account of the
working of the tithe law in the Emperor's territories, so different to the teaching and spirit of the
Gospel! The laity, however, refused to pay the tax.

In England, the *custom* of giving tithes as free-will offerings gradually began, as I stated above,
in the eighth century, or eleven hundred years ago.
The clergy were then quite satisfied with such
voluntary offerings. A few only at first gave
them; then the number gradually increased, by
means of the pressure exercised in the confessional
box, in the ninth, tenth, and eleventh centuries,

until it finally became *customary* for ALL to pay their tithe offerings. The usual question put by the priest from the confessional box was, "If they duly paid their tenths to God?" In A.D. 850, a German bishop in his visitations, had specially this article of inquiry, "Si decimas recte darent?" The custom in England gradually changed into a *common right*, and it was by virtue of this common right that people were legally bound to pay tithes. There was no positive law made for their payment. But here is their injustice. When this *custom* commenced, the population of England and Wales could not have exceeded 750,000, with about a million of acres under cultivation, and yet this *custom*, originating under the above circumstances, generated a *common law right*, which legally bound all subsequent generations to the payment of predial, mixt, and personal tithes. I call this barefaced injustice. It is utter nonsense to state, as some Church defenders do, that all the parochial tithe endowments were voluntarily bestowed on the Church by the landowners. I refer the reader to p. 132 for further remarks on this subject in the "Retrospective View of Tithes in England."

As regards tithes, the pope was the Quarter-Master General of the clerical army. He was the supreme steward of the clergy's maintenance; the ruling and guiding spirit for the payment of tithes.

Certain writers argue in the most unreasonable manner against the division of tithes in England, and assert that the parson was legally entitled to, and had enjoyed, all his tithes without diminution. Lord Selborne, in his recent work, is the latest supporter of this erroneous view. I have fully stated at pp. 27-29, and in chap. xiii., the arguments in favour of the tripartite division of tithes in England.

The Norman monks initiated the appropriation of tithes to monastic bodies. The lands belonging to the four privileged orders were specially exempted from paying tithes, whilst others purchased bulls of exemption from the popes.

The Third and Fourth Lateran Councils held in 1180 and 1215 respectively, issued decrees against infeudations and for the payment of tithes. The latter Council gave the English parson a common right to parochial tithes. General Councils, in which the laity were unrepresented, had no right to pass decrees against the disposition of the private property of the laity to whatever religious purpose they wished, or for the payment of tithes. Their functions were confined to the discipline and doctrines of the Church.

Introduction.

When monasteries were dissolved by 31 Henry VIII., c. 8, and by 1 Edward VI., the tithes as well as the lands of the monasteries passed to the Crown, and the Crown granted them to laymen, whose posterity or assignees hold them up to the present day, and are protected in their possession of the tithes and Church estates by 32 Henry VIII., c. 7. In Edward VI.'s reign about six millions of acres were under cultivation, but from that time to the present, over twenty millions of waste lands have been brought into cultivation for which tithes were paid. From A.D. 1547 to A.D. 1886, about 5000 new parishes have been formed, of which about 3500 were formed this century, and 2500 from A.D. 1547 to A.D. 1800, or an annual average of 10 parishes, compared with an annual average of 40 from 1800 to 1886, or 57 a year from 1832 to 1886.

These facts and figures give a tolerably clear idea of how the Reformed Church of England advanced from A.D. 1547 to A.D. 1800, when the spiritual ministration of the country was decidedly bad and neglected in proportion as the tithes increased. This is exactly what may be expected from tithe-paid clergy, who were freeholders and parochial autocrats for life, subject to no control but that of the bishop, which, in those days, was at its lowest ebb.

The Nonconformists were hard at work when the Church, like the five foolish virgins, was fast asleep. But, towards the end of the first quarter of the present century, there arose a cry for Church Reform. Dr Howley, Archbishop of Canterbury, was the first to have taken steps, in 1829, to reform the then existing abuses in the Established Church, as to episcopal revenues, commendams, non-residence of incumbents, sinecures, pluralities, &c., which were like so many cancers eating away the body politic. This led to Earl Grey's Royal Commission of Inquiry, dated 23rd June 1832; to Sir Robert Peel's Commission, dated 4th February 1835; to the five remarkable ecclesiastical reports of 1835 and 1836; to the Episcopal and Tithe Commutation Acts of 1836; to the Ecclesiastical Commission for England, 1836; to the Pluralities Act of 1838; to the Cathedral Act of 1840; in fine, to the passing, from 1836 to 1886, or fifty years, of about one hundred and twenty statutes directly and indirectly affecting the Church, besides some thousands of Orders in Council, having the force of Acts of Parliament. Yet many churchmen assert that the Church of England has received no help from the State (!) What amount of money would have paid the members of the various Governments from 1832, who boldly stepped for-

Introduction.

ward to drag the State Church out of that sink of abuses in which the first reformed Parliament found her? If the reforming steps had not been taken in 1832 by our leading statesmen, the Church, with all its flagrant abuses, would have been swept away as an Established Church.

The Commutation Act settled a long burning question. The tithe owners obtained four millions of tithe rent charge, and the landlords gained two millions a year by the arrangement, besides paving the way to gradually increased rentals. The landlords have also gained about half a million more per annum by the various changes which were made in the extraordinary tithe charges. But owing to agricultural depression, the tithe owners, if the Commutation Act was not passed, would now be receiving from tithes in kind, if collected and sold, not much more than the gross tithe rent charge. The Church has, therefore, lost nothing at the present time by the Commutation Act. By the Commutation Act, the landlords and not the tenants are the real tithe rent payers. By the landlords contracting themselves out of the 80th clause of that Act, and arranging with the tenants to pay the tithe rent charge, a good deal of ill-feeling has sprung up in certain parts of the country on the part of the farmers against the tithe owners.

The tithe question is one which may finally be settled upon the principle of Redemption. As this is a most important question, I have devoted a whole chapter—XII.—to its consideration. The Redemption of the tithe rent charge is the only feasible solution of a very serious question which is liable to crop up at any time, and to lead to bitter strife between the farmers and the tithe owners.

When Henry VIII. had taken the pope's place as "Supreme head of the Church of England," he made no change in her doctrines, and the clergy received their tithes as hitherto. But in the reigns of his son and Elizabeth, changes were made in both ritual and doctrines; and those incumbents who refused to adopt the new doctrines, framed in accordance with those used in the Primitive Christian Church, were deprived of their incumbencies, and consequently of their tithes and other Church endowments. But there was no physical transfer made then of such endowments, and the Church was the same Church of England, but reformed. Their successors, who embraced the new doctrines and ritual, were appointed on the condition of strictly complying with the Acts of Uniformity, and the doctrines enunciated in the Thirty-Nine Articles. It was in virtue of such compliance that they were put in

Introduction.   xxi

possession of the tithes and other endowments of the Church, but not by any physical transfer of the property, which their predecessors had enjoyed. It was purely a change of tenants, without the least disturbance of the property. The new tenant solemnly engaged to comply with the new Church laws: the old tenant refused to do so, and had, therefore, to leave. That was all.

Within the past fifty years the so-called "Catholic revival" movement in the Church of England commenced. Its principal object, notwithstanding jesuitical casuistry or arguments to the contrary, is to Romanize the Church of England. In ritual there is now no difference between a Roman Catholic Church and one of the Reformed Churches of England, the incumbent of which belongs to the advanced ritualistic school. In doctrine, the "Catholic priest" of the Church of England is on a level with the "Roman Catholic" priest; but the latter acknowledges the pope, the former the queen, although he would prefer the pope, as the head of his Church. That seems to be the only difference. The incumbent is a freeholder for life. He has taken, and still takes, every advantage of his independent parochial autocracy, by introducing ritual and doctrines into the services of his Church at variance with her laws. There is no discipline of any consequence in the Church. There is nobody to control the parochial autocrat. He is a freeholder for life. The bishops are powerless, and the majority of them acquiesce in patent and flagrant violations of ritual and doctrines. And yet these incumbents hold fast to the tithes and other parochial endowments, supplemented, to a great extent, from the "Common Fund" of the Ecclesiastical Commissioners, and from the Bounty Board. As a member of the Church of England, I am not surprised at the hostile attitude of Nonconformists towards the Church, when they see her vast endowments enjoyed by men outwardly professing to be the incumbents of the Reformed Church of England, but who are really enemies in the camp, trying their very best to Romanize the Church, and at the same time to stick fast to her tithes and other endowments. They have not the honesty to leave her communion and go over to the enemy. No, they can carry out their plans and designs more successfully within her ranks, and also enjoy all her endowments, to aid them in accomplishing their nefarious designs.

I fully admit that there was a necessity for a moderate revolution within the Church of England. Fifty years ago, and later, the Church was puritanical and not Anglican. The incumbents and bishops were torpid, indolent, and neglected their spiritual duties. The sacraments were neglected and even desecrated; the church doors were closed from Sunday to Sunday; the services were performed in a cold, irreverent manner; the so-called "Evangelical party" drove their carriage and four through the rubrics, canons, and articles of the Church. But all held a firm grip on their tithes and other endowments, while the spiritual destitution of the masses was really alarming and disgraceful; all that is changed now, and for the better. The revolution came, but, like all revolutions, it was pushed to extremes. A few fanatics crossed the Rubicon on their march to Rome, and burnt their boats. Others followed, until at the present day the number of followers has alarmingly increased. Our people now find it very easy to step from the Church of England into the Church of Rome. That is not so with the Non-Conformists or members of the Church of Ireland or Episcopal or Free Church of Scotland. We never read of any of their ministers or members going over to Rome, but it is a very common thing to read of "verts" to Rome from the clerical and lay ranks of the Church of England. The way to Rome is so well prepared by the clerical agents working within the Church, and enjoying her endowments, that the "verts" find the change to Rome so easy that they perceive no difference whatever between the two Churches. A foolish law gives the bishops the power of vetoing clerical prosecutions. The majority of the bishops sympathise with the extremists, and by virtue of the veto will not give their sanction to prosecutions. The bishops are popularity seekers; they wish to be on good terms with their clergy, and to keep ritualistic scandals in the background, because they know well that the less publicity is given to such scandals the better for the Establishment. The great fault is that there exists no diocesan body to advise and control the bishops, and no parochial body to act similarly over the parochial autocrats and freeholders for life. If the Church were Disestablished, these controlling and ruling bodies would spring up at once into existence, and then there would be the beginning of a healthy revolution, in which the influence and the power of the lay element in the Anglican Church would be felt in every parish and in every diocese throughout the land. The "vert" tide would then be turned back from Rome, and the Anglican members would find sufficient spiritual comfort and consolation within their own old and venerable Church of England, whose doctrines are framed on Holy

Scripture, and not on the errors of a corrupt and a corrupting church.

It is an indubitable fact that the "Catholic Revival" has transformed the Church of England into a *nursery* or recruiting depôt for the Church of Rome; and as years have rolled on, the nursery has been enlarged, its management made more perfect and effective for the object in view, by young ardent incumbents joining the ranks, and pushing the Revival to extremes. All this is carried out by freeholders for life enjoying vast Church endowments, uncontrolled by, and independent of, their parishioners and bishops. England is therefore to be Romanised through and by her National Reformed Church. Convents are built in their parishes with episcopal permission and visitation; ladies with their fortunes are admitted; rules of discipline and doctrines are framed by the incumbents on the lines of those of the Roman Catholic Church. When any of the inmates wish to leave, like Miss Allcard and Miss Stirling of the "Convent of Mary at the Cross," a Protestant (or "Anglican," if preferred) institution in Mark Street, Finsbury, London, the "sisters" step out of the Anglican convent, and pass at once, without hesitation, into the Church of Rome, and no doubt without perceiving any difference between the two churches. [See *Times*, 21st and 22d January 1887, "Allcard *v.* Skinner," heard in the Chancery Division.] One of the rules of the above convent, as given in evidence, is that the voice of the Mother Superior "must necessarily be regarded as the voice of God" (!) Just imagine such a rule for "Sisters" in a Protestant institution, sanctioned and visited by the bishops of the Church of England! How long must this last?

Lord Selborne, in his "Defence of the Church of England," carefully avoids all references to the indubitable fact as regards the existence of this nursery for Rome within the Church, and it is such existence which makes Disestablishment the vital question for the near future. I am no Liberationist *quâ* Liberationist, but, as a sound Churchman, I am totally opposed to seeing the pure Church of England transformed into a nursery or recruiting depôt for the corrupt Church of Rome, and her vast endowments utilised for any such purpose.

How long, then, will the people of England permit their National Reformed Church, with all her endowments, to exist as a nursery for the Church of Rome? Are they prepared to permit the Church to occupy the *status quo ante* Reformation?

How long would the pope and his "Propaganda" at Rome, permit the parish priests of the National Church of any Roman Catholic country, to convert their parishes into nurseries for the propagation of Protestant ritual, discipline, and doctrines? Not one day. They would move heaven and earth at once to smash up the pernicious nurseries, and expel the mutineers from their parishes. There is discipline in the Church of Rome, but none in the Church of England.

I grant that Disestablishment would create a revolution in the Church, on account of the Revival or Romanising movement having been permitted to exist so long. But between two evils, I select the lesser. Disestablishment would disperse the nurseries. Diocesan and Parochial mixed boards of lay and clerical members would control and purify the Church. Diocesan and Parochial autocrats would no longer exist. Stringent codes of discipline would be framed, and short, sharp, and decisive steps would be taken against clerical delinquents. Candidates for Incumbencies, with Romanising tendencies, would find no favour with Boards of Patronage. And if by any chance they were appointed under false colours, and afterwards attempted to form recruiting depôts for Rome, the parishioners would have the power to make their disapproval felt by stopping "supplies" until their grievances were redressed. The lay and clerical members would also have a voice in the selection of their bishops.

HENRY W. CLARKE.

February 1887.

THE HISTORY OF TITHES.

CHAPTER I.

BEFORE THE CHRISTIAN ERA.

THE first instance on record of the payment of tithes is found in Genesis xiv. 20, when Abraham, after having rescued Lot, was returning a victor from the battle with the spoils of war. King Melchizedek met him on the way, and Abraham gave him, in his office of priest of God, "tithes of all." It is a disputed point whether Abraham meant a tithe of all his property, or of all the spoils of war which he had with him.

The next instance we find is the vision of Jacob's ladder. He vowed to God, "Of all that Thou shalt give me, I shall surely give the tenth unto Thee" (Genesis xxviii. 22). It is laid down in the Mosaic Law, "And thou shalt truly tithe all the INCREASE of thy seed that the field brought forth year by year" (Deut. xiv. 22). It is important to note the word "increase" in this passage, which in our law courts had often decided disputed cases, whether certain things were tithable or not. For instance, were all herbs tithable? Only those which man eats. In Leviticus xxviii. 30-32, "All the tithe of the land, whether of seed of the land or of the fruit of the tree, is the Lord's, and the tithe of the herd or of the flock, even of whatsoever passeth under the rod, the tenth shall be holy unto the Lord." It was the custom for a person to be at the sheep-cot with a coloured rod, and as the sheep came out one by one, every tenth was marked with this rod; and that is what is meant by "passing under the rod."

The priests at Jerusalem received the first fruits and heave offerings, but not the tithes. The heave offerings were the one-sixtieth of the gross produce. But the tithes were devoted to the whole tribe of Levi at Jerusalem, and they gave the tithe of their tithes to the priests—that is, one-hundredth part. It was from this custom, and in order to support the Crusades, that the popes of Rome exacted early in the fourteenth century the first fruits and the tithe of the tithes from the hierarchy and beneficed clergy, who were under their spiritual jurisdiction. And when King Henry the Eighth displaced the pope, and assumed the supreme authority in the Church, he also exacted the first fruits and tenths, which went to his favourites.

Before the Christian Era. 3

Queen Anne, by an Act of Parliament passed in 1704, gave them back to the Church for the special purpose of augmenting poor livings.

After the destruction of the second temple and the dispersion of the Jews, the payment of tithes among the Jews had ceased, because they thought that Jerusalem alone was the place where tithes ought to be paid, and also because it became impossible to trace out the tribe and priesthood to whom alone they were to be paid. It is a question whether the Jews, who were converted to Christianity before the destruction of the second temple had paid tithes to the Levites.

The heathen nations seem to have copied and adopted the Jewish custom of paying tithes. We read of the Greeks having paid tithes of the spoils of war to Apollo, and of the Romans to Hercules. But, properly speaking, they were not the sort of tithes mentioned in the Mosaic law. They were only arbitrary vows and offerings; but no conclusion can be drawn that they were tithes because tenths were given. Sometimes the heathen offered more and sometimes less than one-tenth.

Some ardent supporters of the payment of tithes make themselves ridiculous in tracing the origin to Adam! They state that Adam paid tithes. Here is their story. "God charged Adam when there was but one man in the world, that he should give Him the tenth part of everything, and to teach his children to do the same; but as there was no man to receive it for Holy Church, God commanded that the tenth part of everything should be burned. In the offerings of Cain and Abel, Abel tithed truly of the best, but Cain tithed falsely of the worst. Cain killed Abel because he said he tithed evil. So people must see that false tithing was the cause of the first murder, and it was the cause that God cursed the earth" (Selden, p. 169).

It is very wrong that Scriptural passages, such as the one given above, should be distorted in order to induce people to pay tithes to "Holy Church."

CHAPTER II.

FROM THE CHRISTIAN ERA TO A.D. 400.

IN apostolical times the Christian ministers were supported by voluntary contributions. Those who preached the Gospel lived by the Gospel; but this scriptural statement did not mean, as some assert, by the payment of tithes, otherwise it would have been stated. St Paul ordered weekly collections to be made for the saints in the churches of Galatia and Corinth (1 Cor. xvi. 1, 2). The voluntary contributions of the faithful were collected and put into a common treasure (Acts ii. 44; iv. 34). The liberality of the Christians, then, far exceeded anything which could have been collected from tithes. And even if tithes were exacted, it is exceedingly doubtful whether the progress of Christianity would not have been materially checked at its outset.

The Jewish law, as regards the payment of tithes, was not binding upon Christians, no more than the custom of bigamy and polygamy adopted by the Israelites, is binding on the Christian Church. There is no injunction in the New Testament binding Christians to pay tithes to their ministers. And when the payment was first urged in the Christian Church, it was supported by reference to the Mosaic Law and not to St Paul's words, That those who preach the Gospel should live by the Gospel.

The Apostolical Constitutions for the Christian Church, collected, as it is said, by Pope Clement I., were framed many centuries after apostolical times. Cardinal Bellarmine is honest enough to ignore them. Selden, in his "History of Tithes," thinks they were concocted about A.D. 1000; others think 1042. In these Constitutions tithes are stated to have been paid by the Christians to the Apostles. Sir H. Spelman (p. 108) thinks that the first thirty-five canons are very ancient. "Dionysius Exiger," he says, "who lived within 400 years after the Apostles, translated them out of Greek. The fifth canon ordained that first fruits and tithes should be sent to the house of the bishop and priests, and not to be offered upon the altar." The Greek word in the copy is not δεκασμοὺς. No solid argument for the payment of tithes can be founded on this canon, for if we take the custom of the Anglo-Saxon churches at the end of the sixth century, which was in accordance with that in primitive times, we find no account of the payment of tithes.

From the Christian Era to A.D. 400.

The monks in their cells had sufficient leisure to concoct these Constitutions, and palm them on the credulous as having been the genuine production of the Apostles. The concocted Constitutions were copied and handed down from century to century without any attempt being made to test their genuineness and authenticity. It seems exceedingly strange that Anglican divines and laymen should refer to the Apostolical Constitutions as an authority for the payment of tithes in apostolic times, although Bellarmine, a great champion of " Holy Church," ignored them. (See the Animadversion on Selden's " History of Tithes in 1621," by Dr R. Tillesley, Archdeacon of Rochester.)

Churchmen like the Archdeacon, many of whom being in the receipt of tithes or tithe-rent charges, will naturally act like drowning men, and snatch even at passing straws to save the tithes. Could anything, for example, be more childish and absurd than the story of tracing the payment of tithes to Adam? And what makes the case worse, is to distort Scripture so as to deceive the people who could neither read nor write, and even those who could read had no open Bible to consult to see for themselves whether these things were so.

Members of the Anglican Church forget when using such weapons as the " Constitutions " in support of tithes, that the very cause of the English Reformation in the sixteenth century was the adoption into the English Church of the traditions and errors of the Church of Rome, which were said to have been handed down by the Apostles, although many of them can be shown to be contrary to Holy Scripture. Archdeacon Tillesley does not defend the whole volume of the Constitutions of Clement, but he does that part about the payment of tithes. He evidently had forgotten the mechanical axiom, that nothing is stronger than its weakest part. "Because the early Christians," he says, "were liberal to the Church, therefore it was reasonable that tithes in the 'Constitutions Apostolical' were true." Nothing of the sort.

After apostolical times, monthly offerings and oblations, we are informed, were made in all the churches, and were used for three purposes—(1) In maintaining the clergy; (2) in supporting the sick and needy; (3) in repairing the church fabric. These monthly contributions were in the third century augmented by grants of lands, which were annexed to churches. In A.D. 322, Constantine, the first Christian emperor, published an edict, giving full liberty to his subjects to give as large a proportion of their property to the clergy as they should think proper. From all these sources of revenue the Christian Church was increasing in wealth. But for more than four hundred years after the Christian era, there was no authoritative church canon made for the payment of tithes; and then such canon was founded upon the Mosaic Law. The question then is, Are Christians justified in adopting the Mosaic Law for the payment of tithes? This law had no force outside Jewish territory. There is no order in the New Testament for their payment. Among the Jews we fail to find such anomalies, rather scandals, in their payment as are found in England. The tithe-rent charge in 1882 was slightly over four millions per annum. Among the Jews were not to be found lay impropriators receiving annually £766,233; schools, colleges, charities, and hospitals receiving £196,056. Here is nearly a quarter of the tithe-rent charge taken by people who are quite unconnected with the religious duties of those parishes from which the tithes arise. Then, again, we have a large extent of land — formerly monastic land — tithe free. There are also the lands in the vicinity of cities and towns built upon, for which the landlords receive large ground-rents, and, when the leases expire, take possession of the house property. These landlords pay nothing to the church for the increased value of their land except a tithe-rent charge of about ten shillings per acre, although the landlords may, from ground-rents alone, receive one hundred times the yearly value per acre, before it was built upon. This is the injustice of tithes.

In the Christian Church, tithes were FIRST given by the faithful as spontaneous offerings, at the urgent solicitations of the clergy. "Nam nemo compellitur," says Tertullian, "sed sponte confert." These spontaneous tithe free-will offerings were not given in cash but in kind. Some gave a tithe of sheep, others of wool, or of corn, &c., just according to the will of the donor. This was the germ of tithes in the Christian Church, which commenced in the fourth century, and were ordered to be paid by canon law about the beginning of the fifth century. The canons which were framed afterwards had ordered them to be paid as a right, as a divine law of the Old Testament, and were not to be considered as free-will offerings. Here is just that specimen of arbitrary conduct on the part of ecclesiastics which would only be tolerated in the dark and Middle Ages. Tithes were too profitable a source of revenue to be ignored in the Christian Church.

A book entitled, "The Englishman's Brief on behalf of his National Church," has been published by the S.P.C.K. A good cause needs no fiction to support it. In that book there is quite twice as much fiction as facts. The extensive circulation of this mixture has embarrassed many in gaining a correct knowledge of the tithe question from the earliest period to the present time. It is written in the style adopted by special pleaders. It gives but one side of the subject. It contains a long string of questions, as if asked by opponents, and the "Brief" in the hands of a special pleader, answers them *ex parte*, and carefully omits a great deal which could be said on the other side. One side is heard in court, but not the other. I strongly object to this way in dealing with so important a subject as the history of tithes in this country. To be appreciated, the history or "Brief" must be impartial. In court, "Briefs" are usually held by different pleaders on both sides. The S.P.C.K. has handed a "Brief" for one side, that is, the National Church. I do not pretend to hold a "Brief" for the other side. But I hold a "Brief" for both sides. It is not my object to review that book here *seriatim*, and to point out what is fiction and what is fact. In my statements throughout this work, a good deal of the fiction is refuted indirectly without reference to the "Brief." But I feel it absolutely necessary to indicate a few of the remarkable feats of fiction which appear in it. When the Christian Religion was first propagated, the writer would have us believe that the converted Jews transferred the payment of their tithes from the Jewish to the Christian ministers, just as easily and as quietly as a man now could transfer the payment of a cheque from one bank to another. Here are the words of the "Brief":—"So that when the Jews and heathen became Christians, throwing off their old religion and adopting the new religion of Christianity, they never dreamt of being less liberal to that form of religion which they loved the more and had adopted, than they had been toward that which they had loved the less and had discarded. Hence the transfer of tithes from the old religion to the new religion" (p. 34). We are not informed upon what authority this statement is made. There is nothing about it in Josephus. There is no order in the New Testament. We read nothing of this in the writings of the first and second centuries. We read of exhortations to pay tithes in the writings of the third and fourth centuries. We read of canons being made for the first time in the fifth century for their payment. But I have failed to find any evidence to support the statement quoted from the "Brief."

From the Christian Era to A.D. 400.

I shall have occasion again to refer specially as well as indirectly, in some of the other chapters of this work, to the misleading and often fictitious statements contained in the "Brief" put forward by the S.P.C.K.

CHAPTER III.

FROM A.D. 400 TO 787.

THE Provincial Council of French bishops, held at Mascon, A.D. 586, is considered to have been *the earliest council* which ordained the payment of tithes. It ordained, " Ut decimas ecclesiasticas omnis populus inferat, quibus sacerdotes aut in pauperum usum, aut in captivorum redemptionem erogatis, suis orationibus pacem populo ac salutem impetrent." It is strange that Isidore, in his compilation of decrees of councils, makes no reference to this council. Friar Crab is the first to have mentioned it in his edition of the councils under Charles V. (Selden, " History of Tithes," p. 58.) The mistake originated in calling the offerings and oblations, tithes. The same mistake is repeated by writers at the present day when treating on the subject of tithes. For instance, Dr J. S. Brewer, in his book entitled " Endowments and Establishment of the Church of England," second edition, 1885, translates "portiones," quoted from Bede, "tithes." Pope Gregory says in his reply to Archbishop Augustin's question, "Communi autem vita viventibus jam de faciendis portionibus, vel exhibenda hospitalite et adimplenda misericordia, nobis quid erit loquendum." But as for those who live in common, why should we say anything now of making portions? Dr Brewer translates the passage thus—"As for those who are living in common, I need give no advice about dividing TITHES, &c." Now, the Latin word for tithe is "decima," and is so used in all the monastic charters. The same writer states, and he is followed by writers of leaflets for the Church Defence Institution, that the scriptural precept, "To live of the Gospel" (1 Cor. ix. 13), refers to the payment of tithes. I am certain St Paul never intended anything of the sort as a compulsory payment. I fully admit that the passage may cover a tithe free-will offering, the same as any other free-will offering, but I cannot believe it implies a compulsory payment of tithes, that is, to carry it out to its logical sequence, a distraint on the goods of a person who is unable or unwilling to pay the tithe. I hold strongly the view that free-will offerings are the only scriptural mode for the maintenance of the Christian ministers, &c. And it was as free-will offerings they were first given to the Church. I shall show in another part how tithe free-will offerings were made compulsory.

The instances are numerous in which words of old authors and passages of Scripture are not only strained but intentionally distorted in order to show the early origin of tithes. There is nothing gained, but much confidence lost, in this critical age by distorting the meaning of or giving a forced interpretation to plain words of Scripture, or of secular and religious writers.

The Christian religion had been introduced into Britain at a very early date, and from Britain it passed over to Ireland. Ireland was specially remarkable for her evangelical missionary monks who visited Scotland, England, and the Continent for the purpose of converting the heathen. Its geographical position favoured a quiet, retired, and contemplative life. Britain served as a "buffer" for many centuries against the piratical devastations of the northern hordes. The inhabitants of Ireland were therefore left in quiet and undisturbed possession of their lands, churches, and monasteries, at a time when the inhabitants of Britain were driven from the east and south to the west of the island; their lands taken from them, their churches and monasteries pillaged, and then destroyed by the invaders.

Pope Gregory the Great selected Augustin, a Benedictine monk, with forty followers of the same order, to proceed on a mission to Britain in order to convert the pagan Saxons to Christianity. They were not of the strict Benedictine order, who lived according to the rule framed A.D. 529, but rather belonged to an earlier and less severe type. They were almost all laymen. The journey to Britain was then considered a hazardous undertaking, being considered in so remote a part of the world. Even this band of Christian pioneers became disheartened on the journey, and would have returned to Rome had not the pope valiantly urged them to carry out their mission. This forms a grand and noble feature in the character of that good Christian bishop. The bishops of Rome at that period were true exponents of apostolical doctrines as taught in Holy Scripture. We must go to a later period, and even to the present century, when the bishops of Rome were elevated to a position as to their infallibility equal to that of God.

The missionaries landed in the Isle of Thanet A.D. 597. Ethelbert, a heathen, was then King of Kent, but his wife was a Christian princess. The king visited Augustin and his companions in their new island home. He was much impressed with their external ceremonies, and permitted them to reside in Canterbury. He presented his palace there to Augustin as his residence. The king appointed Canterbury as Augustin's episcopal see. There were also in the island some British churches, bishops, and clergy, but there were no divisions of parishes, no parish churches, and certainly no tithes paid. If such had been paid, Bede, in his "Ecclesiastical History," would inform us. I shall show further on that the payment of tithes in England was of foreign importation, some centuries after Augustin's mission. He was consecrated archbishop A.D. 597, and died 605. In 602 he laid the foundation of the cathedral church of Canterbury. In 604 he ordained Mellitus, one of his companions, bishop of London, and Justus, another companion, bishop of Rochester. King Ethelbert granted them London and Rochester respectively as their episcopal sees. These bishops and their clergy (episcopi clerus) were then but missionaries in the country, and being monks, had lived together close to their cathedral churches, from which they proceeded as itinerant preachers to the neighbouring localities. The bishop's church was called the cathedral church, *mater ecclesia*, because the bishop had his cathedra, sedes, bishop-stool or chair, in the choir. The modern grand title is "Bishop's Throne," placed by itself in a conspicuous part of the church. There are only two cathedral churches in England in which the "Throne" is in the choir, but in a raised position. The bishop's circuit or diocese was the parish; hence the terms "parish" and "diocese" were then synonymous. He was therefore the rector and bishop of the parish or diocese. It will be shown further on that the canon law gave the bishop the right to all the tithes in the diocese. The rules and vows of the monks prevented them from being scattered over the diocese. They lived together in common, and within their monastery. Their chief functions were, to instruct the new converts, who, when duly prepared, were sent forth by the bishop as ordained itinerant ministers, to preach to and convert their countrymen in the distant parts of the diocese, where there were no churches, but crosses erected at convenient spots, and around these crosses the people assembled to hear the word of God, to have their children baptized, and to partake of the Sacrament of the Lord's Supper. Collections were always made on such occasions, which the preâchers brought and deposited at the bishop's house for the common fund. When the itinerant preachers—episcopi clerus—saw people eager and zealous in their religious duties, they reported the same to the bishop, who had caused to be built for them, out of the common fund, wooden chapels or churches. These served as chapels of ease to the mother church. In some cases the bishop had a house constructed close to the chapel or church, where a priest could permanently reside. The bishops had the advowsons of all such churches. The nobility and landed gentry were not slow in fully appreciating the advantages of resident to itinerant priests. They also felt the great inconvenience, especially in winter, of attending services at the cathedral church, which may be at a considerable distance from their residences. The villagers were even in a worse condition. So the landowners slowly commenced about A.D. 650, and most actively just after A.D. 700, to build churches upon their estates, the parochial limits of which were made conterminous with the extent of their properties, hence we find some of the old parishes of very unequal extent. The churches were for the use of the landowners' families, servants, tenants, and labourers. Residences for the priests were built close to the churches, and the landowners endowed the incumbents with glebe lands for their maintenance, but there is no evidence to show that the landowners at that early period endowed them with the tithes of their properties. The ministers had therefore for their maintenance the glebe lands and a part of the offerings of the congregations. The people who dwelt upon the property had the right to worship in the church thus built for them by the landowner without payment for seats, which is a modern custom dating from the Church Building Acts passed early in the present century. From these statements three salient facts are to be observed. (1.) Churches were built and endowed by the landowners, but not with tithes. (2.) Parish churches commenced to be built about A.D. 650. (3.) Parochial boundaries commenced to be formed about A.D. 675 or A.D. 700. The endowments at first consisted of (*a*) the church, (*b*) the parsonage, and (*c*) the glebe lands. To these a fourth was subsequently added, viz., tithes.

As the population of the country increased, and the parish churches were far away from towns where large populations congregated, new churches had to be built within the parochial limits for their convenience. The founder, and not the rector of the mother church, had to give his assent to the erection of the daughter church, but the rector presented the new incumbent to the bishop for institution. King Edgar, as will be seen further on, ordered that every such daughter church, provided it had a cemetery, should receive a third of the tithes of the whole parish, the remaining two-thirds going to the rector.

Why did the vicar receive one-third of the tithes? Because it was the priest's share. This statement is an additional proof of the tripartite division of the tithes, one-third being the rector's.

Edgar's law gave a great impetus to the creation of many small parishes in England; for every proprietor of bocland wished to have a priest on his estate. Each new church, in the course of time, obtained a parochial limit of its own, and enjoyed the profits which the mother church had possessed out of the land included within this limit. The capellæ or chapels of ease, without burial grounds, were differently treated, and therefore had never trenched upon the profits of the parish church. (Selden, pp. 265-267.)

The church built by a layman had to be consecrated by the bishop, but the layowner had the advowson or nomination of the incumbent. This was the origin of lay patronage in the Church of England. The church so built belonged to the manor or estate. When in course of time the property was sold or otherwise disposed of, the advowson went with the property. With change of hands the advowson was, by some owners, separated from the manor or estate, and sold to the highest purchaser. The original patron never anticipated this change. It was this separation that has caused the scandalous traffic in church livings. The advowson is now the property of one person, and the manor is the property of another. The sale of the living or advowson is treated on the same footing as the sale of land, houses, &c. The traffic is carried on at public auctions, and the advowson is sold to the highest bidder. Again, some will not sell the advowsons, but the next presentations. The living is worth, say, £800 a year from tithe rent charge, the incumbent is old, and the owner of the advowson is desirous of finding some person who will buy the next nomination when the present incumbent will die. It is a speculation, for it is a life interest which is purchased. In these transactions—this traffic in souls—which have produced most lamentable scandals, private agents, who make this traffic in livings a special branch of their business, carry out the private arrangements between the buyer and seller. All these objectionable proceedings were never anticipated by the original owner, but as the advowson was attached to the estate, it became to have a money value when the property passed into other hands. Many patrons of livings are Roman Catholics, Jews, and infidels. There are owners of advowsons who never sell them, but nominate to their vacant livings the best clergymen they can get, but the large majority of owners of advowsons treat them as private property, and make the most money they can out of them, either by selling the advowsons or selling next presentations. In these few remarks I merely give a brief sketch of the existing scandals as regards the traffic carried on in the sale of livings. For full particulars the reader must consult the proceedings, which appear in the "Parliamentary Papers," vol. xviii., for 1880, p. 379, &c., of Select Committee appointed by Parliament to investigate the whole subject.

The bishops and clergy at first lived together, and were supported by the offerings and oblations of their flocks, which were brought to the bishop's house and put into one common fund for the support (1) of the bishop and his clergy, (2) for the repairs of the church, and (3) for the poor and sick.

The first question which Augustin asked Pope Gregory was, "Into how many portions were the things given by the faithful to the altar to be divided?" (Bede, "Ecclesiastical History," book i. c. 27). He answered, that they were to be divided into four portions (ut in omni stipendio, quod accidit, quatuor debuit fieri portiones), viz., one for the bishop and his family (una episcopo et familiae propter hospitalitatem atque susceptionem), because of hospitality and entertainments, another for the clergy, a third for the poor, and a fourth for the repair of churches. Gregory advised Augustin, however, to adopt the custom of the Anglo-Saxon Church, which was, he said, in accordance with the use adopted in primitive times, viz., to have all things in common among them. In both question and answer we do not find one word about tithes.

The quadripartite division of the common fund mentioned by Pope Gregory, existed only in the diocese of Rome, and commenced at the end of the fifth century. In France, Spain, and other countries, the tripartite division existed, by combining the first and second.

In England, the bishops and "episcopi clerus" lived in common until about A.D. 700, when the custom commenced to cease. The Anglo-Saxon kings lavishly endowed the bishops with real estates. Up to 705 there were nineteen bishops in England and Wales. As the Episcopal endowments increased, the bishops became more independent, and therefore, in 700, we find them separating themselves from their clergy, and living on the profits of their estates. But they also received their shares of the common fund, which continued until the eleventh century, when by canon law they were prohibited from participating in the common fund and tithes. The parochial clergy then took the place of the bishops, and divided the tithes into three parts—one they kept for themselves, a second was distributed in charity, and a third was set aside for repairing and decorating the churches. I am aware that this tripartite division of tithes in England is denied, and it is asserted that the rectors received their tithes in full as a common right, and were not bound to make any provision out of them for charity or repairs of the churches. But after carefully studying the question, I can perceive no reason why I should change my opinion. The writers who deny this division, admit that the rector's common right grew out of the custom of free-will offerings of tithes.

This admission upsets the denial, for it can be shown that the original custom never gave all the tithes to the parson on the Continent or in England.

The following are my reasons for adhering to the opinion that a tripartite division of tithes existed in England, or that some division existed, and that the rector had not the enjoyment of all the tithes :—

1. When at the end of the fourth and beginning of the fifth century, some of the prominent bishops of the Christian Church, especially Augustin of Hippo, in his sermon, "De Tempore," first strongly urged the payment of tithes, it was in order that the wants of the poor may be attended to.

2. In reply to Augustin's letter, Pope Gregory states that all the emoluments must be divided into four portions, of which the clergy received but one. When tithes were given as free-will offerings, like other church contributions, the pope's statement clearly indicates that the clergy did not receive all the tithe free-will offerings. The argument is the same where the tripartite system was in use.

3. In the collection of canons attributed to Archbishop Egbert, it is stated that the priest should divide the tithes into three parts, one of which the priest was to keep for himself. Although this collection bears internal evidence of having been compiled some centuries after the archbishop's death, yet it shows that a tripartite division of the tithes must have been made in England at the time the collection was formed, otherwise the compiler or compilers would not have mentioned the division as having existed in Egbert's time, meaning his or their own time. There is a remarkable statement in the canons attributed to Egbert, that the priest

was to make a distribution of the tithes "coram testibus." Now, the distribution of the tithes had passed through the priest's hands, and "coram testibus" was to prevent him from taking too large a proportion for his own use.

4. See page 22.

5. A law of Ethelred in 1013. In a constitution of his there appears the following :—"Concerning tithes that the King and his Witan have decided and pronounced, even as the law is, that one-third of the tithes of every church shall go to the repair of the church, one-third to the servants of God, and one-third to God's poor and to necessitous persons in servitude." This is but a declaratory law, a confirmation of the common law of the land. There is no foundation for the assertion that this law, attributed to Ethelred, is not genuine.

6. In his letter, about A.D. 1200, to the Archbishop of Canterbury, enjoining the payment of tithes to the parsons of parishes, Pope Innocent III. declared it to be a grievous sin to give the tithes and first fruits to the poor and not to the priests. From this we may reasonably infer that a proportion, and not all, of the tithes and first fruits was at that time devoted to the support of the poor, and thus keeping up the ancient custom. This pope was all for the priests and the supremacy of

the See of Rome. His name is associated with one of the most humiliating events in English history.

7. An Act was passed in the reign of Richard II., directing the bishops to ordain a competent sum to be distributed among the poor parishioners annually. Blackstone makes the following remark upon this Act :—" It seems the people were frequently sufferers by the withholding of those alms for which, among other purposes, the payment of tithes was originally imposed." Here is the evidence of a most distinguished and learned judge that it was originally intended that the wants of the poor were to be supplied out of the tithes.

See Chapter xii. for additional information.

Tithe-owners are at present in the enjoyment of all the tithes, or tithe-rent charges, instead of one-third. Those who possess the rectorial tithes keep the chancels in repair. They say they pay poor-rates on the income derived from tithes. They certainly do not pay one-third. They complain that no such burden is placed on the landlords for their rents. I admit that this distinction should not exist. But landlords pay property-tax.

About A.D. 700, three important changes occurred. (1.) The bishops and their clergy discontinued living together. (2.) The parochial system commenced. (3.) The first attempt was made to prevent the clergy from marrying. This last change was gradually brought about by the influence of the Roman Church over the national churches of other countries, and by the monastic orders scattered through these countries in their several monasteries. The influence of the Roman See over the English Church commenced with Augustin's mission, and gradually increased under the Anglo-Saxon kings. About 787 the power of the pope was acknowledged in England, and as supreme head of the Church he exercised the undisputed right of consecrating bishops. It became formidable at and after the Norman Conquest, and reached its zenith in the reign of King John. The order for the celibacy of the clergy in the Church of England was not generally observed for a considerable time after A.D. 700. It gradually gained ground especially during the archiepiscopacy of Dunstan (959-988). But Hildebrand, in the reign of William I., issued special decrees against clerical marriages, which were vigorously carried out in the Church of England. In 1547, the clergy were again permitted to marry, but the Act was repealed by Queen Mary, which her sister could never be induced to repeal again, for Elizabeth was as hostile to clerical marriages as the pope himself. However, in the first year of King James I., the statute of Mary was explicitly repealed.

CHAPTER IV.

FROM A.D. 787 TO 1000.

THE first public lay law decreeing the payment of tithes was made, A.D. 787, by Charlemagne. On this subject I thought it best to quote a remarkable passage from Milman, vol. ii., p. 292, &c.: "On the whole body of the clergy, Charlemagne bestowed the legal claim to tithes. Already, under the Merovingians, the clergy had given significant hints that the law of Leviticus was the perpetual law of God. Pepin had commanded the payment of tithes for the celebration of peculiar litanies during a period of famine. Charlemagne made it a law of the empire; he enacted it in its most strict and comprehensive form as *investing the clergy in a right to the tenth of the substance and of the labour alike of freemen and serf.* The collection of tithes was regulated by compulsory statutes; the clergy took note of all who paid or refused to pay; four or eight or more jurymen were summoned from each parish as witnesses for the claims disputed; the contumacious were three times summoned; if still obstinate, they were excluded from the church; if they still refused to pay, they were fined over and above the whole tithe, six solidi; if further contumacious, the recusant's house was shut up; if he attempted to enter it, he was cast into prison to await the judgment of the next plea of the crown. The tithe was due on all produce, even on animals. The tithe was usually divided into three portions; one for the maintenance of the church, the second for the poor, the third for the clergy. The bishop sometimes claimed a fourth. He was the arbiter of the distribution; he assigned the necessary portion for the church, and appointed that of the clergy. This tithe was by no means a spontaneous votive offering of the whole Christian people. *It was a tax imposed by imperial authority and enforced by imperial power.* It had caused one, if not more than one, sanguinary insurrection among the Saxons. It was submitted to in other parts of the Empire, not without strong reluctance. Even Alcuin ventures to suggest that if the Apostles of Christ had demanded tithes, they would not have been so successful in the propagation of the Gospel."

Mr Hallam says: "Charlemagne was the first who gave the confirmation of a civil statute to these ecclesiastical injunctions. No one, at least as far as I know, adduced any earlier law for the payment of tithes than one of his capitularies" ("Middle Ages," vol. ii., p. 143).

In the same year, 787, Pope Adrian I. sent two legates to England to attend the Synod of Chalchyth (generally supposed to be Chelsea), where they strongly urged the payment of tithes according to the Mosaic Law. These were the first legates sent by the pope to England since Augustin's mission, a period of one hundred and ninety years. Bishop Stubbs, in his "Constitutional History of England," says: "In 787 tithe was made *imperative* by the legatine councils held in England, which, being attended and confirmed by the kings and ealdormen, had the authority of Witenagemots" (vol. i., p. 228).

Here then are some solid historical facts and not fictions for our guidance. The influence of the Roman Church over the English Church for about two hundred years was then being felt. In 597, when Augustin landed on our shores, the Roman Church had no power or influence in England. It was not so in 787, when legates of that church had for the first time visited this country. Then its influence and authority were such that, according to the statement of Bishop

Stubbs, quoted above, tithes were made *imperative by legatine councils* held in England in the year 787. He says the payment of tithes was made *imperative*. This is a strong expression. It is one thing to command them to be paid, it is another thing to make the people obey such command. I am of opinion that they were given as voluntary offerings, and the priests and bishops were glad to receive them as such.

Seven years after the meeting of this synod, viz., 794, Offa, King of Mercia (755 to 796), made a law granting the tithes of his whole kingdom to the Church. It is necessary to briefly state why he made this law. In his cupidity for an increase of territory, he caused Ethelbert, King of the East Angles, to be murdered while sojourning at his court as a suitor for his daughter. In 793 he seized Ethelbert's kingdom, and afterwards made a journey, or rather a pilgrimage, to Rome to obtain the pope's pardon for his cruel act. The pope granted him a pardon on condition that he would be liberal to the clergy. On his return to England, he made the above law in order to atone for his crime. The cause of granting the tithe of his kingdom was not creditable to the Church, nor could such a grant, under the circumstances, be acceptable to God.

I pass over Archdeacon Tillesley's fiction that "Ethelbert and his Parliament gave tithes upon the preaching of Augustin, the monk, about two hundred years before Ethelwulph" ("Animadversions on Mr Selden's 'History of Tithes,'" p. 186).

The next case of granting tithes in England was the law of Ethelwulph, passed in 855 at a general council or Witenagemot, which met at Winchester, and was composed of bishops and lay nobility. Here Ethelwulph, a weak-minded and superstitious prince, who called himself in the charter King of the West Saxons, but was really king of all England, with the two tributary kings of Mercia and East Angles, made a law by and with the advice of his Witan, granting tithes to the Church from all England, and not from his own estates alone. As this is supposed by some eminent writers to be the first law relating to tithes for all England, it is important to give a translation of the charter from Prideaux, chapter iv., p. 110.

A Translation of Ethelwulph's Charter granting Tithes.

"I, Ethelwulph, King of the West Saxons, by the advice of my bishops and other chief men of my kingdom, have resolved on a wholesome and uniform remedy, that is, that I grant as an offering unto God, and the Blessed Virgin, and all the saints, a certain portion of my kingdom to be held by perpetual right, that is to say, the tenth part thereof, and that this tenth part be privileged from temporal duties and free from all secular services and all royal tributes, as well the greater as the lesser, or those taxes which we call Witerden; and that it be free from all things else, for the health of my soul and the pardon of my sins, to be applied only to the service of God alone, without being charged to any expedition, or to the repair of bridges, or the fortifying of castles, to the end that the clergy may with the more diligence pour out their prayers to God for us without ceasing, in which we do in some part receive their service.

"These things were enacted at Winchester, in the Church of St Peter, before the great altar, in the year of the Incarnation of our Lord, 855, in the third indiction, on the nones of November, for the honour of the glorious Virgin and mother of God, St Mary, and St Michael the archangel, and of the blessed Peter, prince of the Apostles, and also of our blessed father, Pope Gregory, and of all the saints.

"These were present and subscribing hereto, all the archbishops and bishops of England, as also Boerred, King of Mercia, and Edmund, King of the East Angles, and also a great multitude of abbots, abbesses, dukes, earls, and noblemen of the whole land, as well as of the other Christian people, who all approved of the royal charter, but those only who were persons of dignity subscribed their names to it.

"King Ethelwulph, for the greater firmness of the grant, offered this charter upon the altar of St Peter the Apostle, and the bishops, on God's part, received the same of him, and afterwards sent it to be published in all the churches throughout their respective dioceses."

The population of England and Wales at this time could not have exceeded 750,000, with a million of acres under cultivation. The tithe in England was only then in its infancy.

The object of the king's charter, according to Ingulph, was to make a general grant of tithes payable as a *free-will offering*. Selden expresses a doubt on Ingulph's construction of this charter. The granting of the tenth part of the hides or plough lands denotes the tenth part of all the profits growing in them. (Selden, p. 206. Decimam omnium hydarum infra regnum suum a tributis et exactionibus regis liberam Deo donavit.)

At that early period in the history of our country, laws were not passed by representative assemblies, and in the same form as they are now. The Witenagemot, or national assembly, was not a representative body like our Parliament. It consisted of bishops, abbots, ealdormen, nobles, and wise men of the kingdom. The great body of ceorls, whose social position was between the thanes and serfs, had not the smallest share in the deliberations of the Witenagemot. The national assembly was therefore a small body, and met when and where the king wished. The bishops and abbots had generally taken the most prominent part in the Witenagemot.

It is asserted by some writers that Ethelwulph had only subjected the royal demesnes to the payment of tithes from which they were exempted before. I cannot endorse this statement.

I have already pointed out the influence of the Roman Church in England—(1) at the Synod of Chalchyth in 787; (2) over King Offa after his pilgrimage to Rome; and now we may observe the same influence at work when (3) King Ethelwulph, in 853, made a pilgrimage with his son Alfred to Rome, where he lived twelve months, devoting his time in devotional exercises. He returned to England in 854, and we can see by his tithe law of 855 what effect Roman influence had over his weak and superstitious mind.

There was no punishment stated in the charter in case of disobedience, and this fact indicates that the tithes were to be given voluntarily. The bishops and priests were perfectly well satisfied with the voluntary gifts which at first were given only by a few individuals. But as time advanced and ecclesiastical influence increased, the clergy used all their spiritual power to increase the number of individuals, and were so successful that the nation, then not numbering more than three-quarters of a million of people, gradually acquiesced in the *custom*, which afterwards became *a common right*, and, like many other customs, formed a part of the common law of England. So the payment of tithes here had been made by common law and not by any positive statute.

Ethelwulph's law of tithes was confirmed by his son Alfred, A.D. 900; by Athelstan, 930; Edmund, 940; Edgar, 970; Ethelred, 1010; Canute, 1020; by the Confessor, William I., and his successors. These confirmations merely gave force to the custom, and to the demands of the clergy for the payment of tithes. They also established the common law right. But it is not known when this common right of the parson commenced. In King John's reign the practice still existed of laymen appropriating the whole of the tithes, or two or three parts to whatever monasteries or churches they wished.

I think this would be a convenient place to define the term "tithe," and to state the various sorts of tithe.

Tithe is "the tenth part of the INCREASE yearly arising and renewing from the profits of lands, the stock upon lands, and the personal industry of the inhabitants" (Blackstone).

Predial tithes are the crops and wood which grow and issue from the ground. Mixt tithes are wool, sheep, cattle, pigs, and milk. They are called mixt because they are predial in respect of the ground on which the animals are fed, and personal from the care they require. Personal tithes are the tenth part of the clear gain after charges were deducted; in other words, on net profits of artificers, merchants, carpenters, smiths, masons, and all other workmen. Even the servant-girls paid a tenth of their wages. The main scriptural passage quoted in support of personal tithes is Deut. xii. 6—"And thither ye shall bring your tithes and heave offerings of your hand."

By 2 and 3 Edward VI., cap. 13, sec. 7, "Every person exercising merchandizes, bargaining and selling clothing, handicraft or other art or faculty, by such kind of persons and in such places as heretofore within these forty years have accustomably used to pay such personal tithes, or of right ought to pay, other than such as be common day labourers, shall yearly, before the feast of Easter, pay for his personal tithes the tenth part of his clear gains, his charges and expenses, according to his estate, condition, or degree, to be therein abated, allowed, and deducted." Sec. 9—" And if any person refuse to pay his personal tithes in form aforesaid, that then it shall be lawful to the ordinary of the diocese, where the party that soe ought to pay the said tithes is dwelling, to call the same party before him, and by his discretion to examine him by all lawful and reasonable means otherwise than by the party's own corporal oath, concerning the true payment of the said personal tithes." Sec. 12 —" Except the inhabitants of the city of London, Canterbury, and the suburbs of the same, and also those of any other town or place that used to pay their tithes by their houses, otherwise than they ought or should have done before the making of this Act."

Sir Robert Philimore states in his "Ecclesiastical Law," p. 1537, that this Act restrained the canon law in three ways. 1. Where the canon law was general that all persons in all places should pay their personal tithes, the Act restrains it to such kind of persons only as have accustomably, that is, constantly, used to pay the same within forty years before the making of the Act. 2. By the ecclesiastical law, the bishop, before the time of this Act, might examine the party upon oath; but this Act restrains that course, so that the party cannot be examined upon oath. 3. By this Act the day labourer is freed from the payment of his personal tithes.

Personal tithes are not now paid in England, except for mills or fish caught at sea, not by the tenth fish, but by a small money payment, and then payable only where the party hears divine service and receives the sacraments.

Predial tithes were claimed on the gross value; personal on the net. Tithes were also divided into "great" and "small." The former were so called because they yielded tithes in greater quantities. The latter were so called because they were produced in smaller quantities. The law, however, has settled the definition by applying the terms to the nature and quality, and not to quantity. (Philimore, p. 1485.) As a general rule, the rector took the "great" tithes, the vicar the "small," but sometimes we meet with a few exceptions to this rule.

As the tithe is the tenth part of the increase from

the land, then coal, lead, and tin mines, slate and stone quarries, turf, tiles, &c., are not tithable, because they are not the *increase* of the land, but part of the freehold, viz., the substance of the earth. Houses in towns and cities are not tithable, because they have no annual *increase* of the soil. Things wild by nature are not tithable, such as the fish of the sea or of rivers. But custom in all or any of the above cases may establish the tithe. (Philimore, p. 1483, &c.)

The modus decimandi, commonly called "modus," was this, that some fixed sum of money or quantity of corn, or other tithable goods, was taken by the tithe-owner instead of taking tithes upon every tithable article. This fixed sum or quantity was termed a *modus*. The customary tithes paid in the city of London is in the nature of a modus. (Philimore, p. 1502.) The Bishop of Exeter had tithes from tin mines of Cornwall. Sometimes a compensation in work or labour was given, so that the parson shall only have the twelfth cock of hay and not the tenth, in consideration of the owner's making it for him. In fine, a modus decimandi is any arrangement by which the general law of tithing is altered and a new method introduced.

It is important to note the following laws made

by King Edgar, who reigned from 959 to 975, and was the re-founder of about forty monasteries :—

(1.) Let every tenth part be returned to the mother church to which the parish is adjacent, of lands, of Thanes, and Villans.

(2.) If any Thane has a church in his fee where there is a cemetery, let him give it the third part of his tithe. [The remaining two-thirds were given to the mother church of the parish.]

(3.) If there is no cemetery there, let him give the priest out of his nine parts what he wishes. [In this case the whole of the tithe went to the mother church, and the Thane had, in addition, to pay something to the priest.]

(4.) If any man should refuse payment of his tithes, as we have said, let the bailiff of the king and of the bishop and the parson of that church meet, and let restitution be made by force to that church to which the tithe belongs, and let them send away the ninth part to him who detained his tithe, and let them divide the eight parts, one-half to the lord of the manor, and the other half to the bishop.

These, with other acts of King Edgar, clearly indicate the powerful influence Archbishop Dunstan had over him.

The second law quoted above was of great importance. If it were carried out at the present day, the several daughter churches which have burial grounds would receive a share of the tithes enjoyed by the parish church. These district or daughter churches relieve the mother church of a large part of the spiritual duties of the parish. But the rector has some thousands a year, while the incumbents of the district churches, carved out of the parish, have each probably less than £250 a year. The mother church should be bound to give a decent maintenance to her offspring. There is no doubt that this arrangement would chime in with the original intentions of the person who endowed the mother church with the tithes of the parish. But here is the difficulty. £1,641,277 rectorial tithes are kept by lay impropriators, bishops, chapters, colleges, schools, charities, and hospitals. They will surrender no part of the tithe rent charge, except they are compelled by law, in order to augment the stipends of incumbents of the daughter churches. Again, there is a large number of resident rectors enjoying from £1000 to £3500 a year, while the incumbents of the daughter churches within their parochial limits have very small stipends. These facts point to a reform in the distribution of parochial revenues.

Parliament could empower the Ecclesiastical

Commissioners to collect all the tithe rent charge, and redistribute the same. They had received such power as regards the episcopal and capitular properties. But these properties and the tithe property are held on different tenures. Some thousands of private patrons have to be dealt with. To divide all the property equally, as some suggest, among the incumbents is purely socialism. May not the properties of laymen be similarly divided? Only twenty-six bishops and thirty cathedral bodies had to be dealt with as regards the episcopal and capitular endowments, which cannot be said to be private property. But it will be a most difficult matter to deal with the various interests of so many thousands of private owners of parochial property. The matter will require great caution and delicate treatment, because there is so much private property concerned.

CHAPTER V.

FROM A.D. 1000 TO 1215.

FROM A.D. 1000 to 1215 is a remarkable period in the history of the English Church and English monasteries. Monasteries were built and richly endowed with lands, churches, and tithes, either in whole or part. All these were conveyed by deeds of gifts to the perpetual use of certain monasteries. The benefactions were given for the special purpose of prayers being perpetually said by the monks in their respective churches for the repose of the souls of the donors and their relatives. In many cases the monasteries received only the tithes, without any churches; but when they received churches, with the cure of souls, then the monastic corporations became the rectors, and, in later times, but not at first, were bound to get the licence of the king and bishop to complete the scheme, so that their corporations may become perpetual incumbents. For many centuries the gifts were conveyed by layowners, without any reference to the king or bishop, for they were considered as private property, which the owner may dispose of to whom he wished. This was afterwards changed, and a licence had to be obtained, as I have previously stated.

The Norman monks, after the Conquest, had first introduced the custom of appropriating the tithes, with the churches, to the monastic corporations. It was another piece of monkish trickery and cunningness to get money, and lands, and buildings. When they gained possession of the churches, with their tithes, either by free gifts or by the purchase of advowsons,—for the monks invested largely in such purchases,—they found it very profitable. As religious services had to be performed in the church appropriated to the monastery, the monastic body had either to depute one of their own fraternity in Holy Orders to do the duty, or appoint a deputy or vicar to act for them at a most miserable stipend. This latter alternative became the general rule. But the abbot or prior took care to get the lion's share of both tithes and parochial offerings.

The capitular chapters, nuns, and religious military orders imitated the practice of the monks, and received similar licences from the king or bishop. In the old appropriations of churches and tithes, the owners considered they were transferring a freehold property, and therefore thought the matter did not require the bishop's confirmation. The patron conveyed the gift by placing the deed and a knife or cup upon the altar of the church of the monastery, as this was then the usual mode of livery of seisin. In the deeds of conveyances, some are given "Canonicis ibidem Deo servientibus," &c.; others, " Canonicis regularibus ibidem Deo servientibus," &c.; and, " Monachis ibidem Deo servientibus," &c.

It is stated in the Acts of the Third Lateran Council of A.D. 1179-80, " So far has the boldness of laymen been carried, that they collate clerks to churches without institution from the bishops, and remove them at their will; and, besides this, they commonly dispose as they please of the possessions and goods of churches." This council condemned the "arbitrary consecrations," as Selden calls them, of laymen. "Before the Council of Lateran (evidently the Third), any man might give his tithes to what spiritual person he would " (Coke's Reports, part ii. p. 44 (*b*).) Four English bishops sat at this council. Alexander III. was then pope. This council gave the death-blow to the arbitrary appropriations of tithes by laymen to whatever church or monastery they pleased. Some had given their tithes to parish churches, but from A.D. 1066 to A.D. 1200 they were all given to monasteries and capitular corporations, none to parish churches. The decree of this council making void arbitrary appropriations of tithes was at first opposed by the laymen of England, and so the practice continued. But the English hierarchy, from that time, opposed the practice, and by degrees it gradually ceased.

Pope Innocent III., in a decretal epistle which he sent to the Archbishop of Canterbury about A.D. 1200, owing to the continued arbitrary appropriation of tithes by laymen in face of the decrees of the Third Lateran Council, enjoined the payment of tithes to the parsons of the respective parishes. But that epistle had no binding force on the lay subjects of this kingdom.

The arbitrary appropriations of tithes by laymen to monasteries, although according to their rights, were contrary to canon law. At a national synod held at Westminster in 1125 (25 Henry I.), it was constituted that no abbot, prior, monk, or clergyman should accept a church or title, or any other ecclesiastical benefice, from a layman without the authority and assent of his own bishop. The lay patrons paid no attention to this canon, because they thought it was an ecclesiastical encroachment upon the rights of property. It was a part of the supremacy over the civil power which the church was then usurping wherever she found weak instruments. However, in the reigns of Richard I. and John, laymen's investitures gradually ceased. The Church became supreme. Archbishop Anselm was a great stickler for papal canons which inhibited the custom of lay investiture. The struggle continued after his death. The practice at the present time is, the patron nominates or presents, the bishop institutes, and the archdeacon inducts. But before the reigns of Richard I. and John, the lay-patrons nominated, instituted, and inducted. The bishop had no voice in the matter. This practice was condemned and made void by the Third Lateran Council of 1180.

At the General Council of Lateran, held in 1215, the arbitrary appropriation of tithes to monasteries or other ecclesiastical corporations which were not parochial was strongly condemned, and the tithes were commanded in future to be paid to the parish churches. This council therefore gave the parsons the parochial right to tithes. It certainly did appear very wrong and even wicked to enrich ecclesiastical bodies with the tithes, and ignore the parochial clergy who did the work, and who were living in a very poor state. But we find that when the parsons received the tithes they became wealthy, indolent, and vicious. We have the testimony of Wickliffe for this statement. No man could write or speak stronger than he did against the conduct of the monks and secular clergy of his time.

In King John's reign the papal power was supreme in England, and therefore the canon law gained strength as England became weak, particularly after Pope Innocent III. issued his interdict against the kingdom.

The decrees of the Council of Lateran, A.D. 1215, had not disturbed the then existing appropriations of tithes to monasteries, but were directed towards the future, and made void all new grants of tithes to monasteries after the date of this council. This council is a landmark for the following arrangements. (1.) The tithes of parishes which, before 1215, could be given by the owners of the property to any church they pleased either in or out of the kingdom, were henceforth to be given only to the parsons of the parishes from which they arose. (2.) The tithes which had been appropriated to persons out of the parishes were continued to be given to them. (3.) The tithes which the parsons possessed before 1215 could not be appropriated afterwards to any other persons. Therefore the tithes which rectors received were those which they possessed at the date of this council, and all tithes created after 1215. The parish system, which commenced

From A.D. 1000 to 1215. 53

about A.D. 700, was completed about A.D. 1200, covering a period of five hundred years. It is supposed that the whole of England was then divided into parishes, and that each parish had its own clergyman. These parishes were gradually formed without any act of the king or of his Witenagemot.

Every man was compelled to pay tithes of his property, but was free to give them to whatever religious body he pleased, either in or out of the kingdom. The Council of Lateran restricted the tithe-payers to the payment of tithes to the parsons of parishes alone. Hence it was designated the parson's common right, which had not been previously enforced. So we may trace tithes (1) as free-will offerings, (2) compulsory payment to some religious body, (3) compulsory payment only to the incumbents of parishes. It is an error to state that all the tithes of England were given freely to the Church; I have stated enough to show that it was not so. The papal power which ignominiously took possession of England and gave it back to King John, to be held by him as a vassal to that Church, was the same power which gave parsons parochial rights to tithes, and deprived laymen of their rights over the disposal of their own property. Pope Alexander III., and especially Innocent III., carried out Hildebrand's scheme of supremacy over the civil powers.

Tithes appropriated to monasteries were of two kinds—(1) Monastical, (2) Parochial. With reference to the first, the monastic bodies performed no spiritual functions for the tithes which benefactors had granted them out of demesnes which had no churches annexed. They had also what is called "pensions," that is, a part of the tithes of some parishes, the remainder going to the resident parish priest. The monastic bodies considered they did their duty for these tithes in distributing alms to the sick, the poor, and the stranger who called at their gates; and also in saying masses perpetually in their churches for the souls of their founders and benefactors, and those of their heirs and other relatives.

As regards the second case, they received churches with tithes annexed as a free gift from the owners, and had the cure of souls. They purchased the advowsons of other churches. They appointed and paid resident vicars for the performance of the spiritual duties of the parishes. But how did they remunerate the vicars? They paid them what they liked; and as the salaries were not fixed, they were varied from year to year as it suited the caprices of the monks, who received all the offerings and oblations given by the faithful to their churches. The vicars' wretched salaries produced great scandal and complaints. The preaching friars and John Wickliffe opened the people's eyes as to the monastic luxuries and the poverty of the vicars whom they employed to do their work. The age of building monasteries and granting extravagant endowments had passed, never to be revived, but there was a growing tendency to sweep them all away. The niggardly manner in which the monks and other ecclesiastical bodies paid their vicars induced Parliament to pass an Act in 1392 (15 Richard II. c. 6), "That the bishops should ordain a competent sum, in proportion to the wealth of the church, to be distributed among the poor parishioners annually, and that the vicar should be sufficiently endowed." Innocent III. complained about A.D. 1200 that the poor instead of the priests received the tithes. Two hundred years after, Parliament had to interfere in the interests of the poor. What do these facts indicate? That parish priests kept not only the tithes but the offerings of the people for their own use, and that the other religious bodies squeezed all the "great tithes" and offerings of the appropriated parishes, without making any provision for the poor. The second point in the Act of 1392 was the miserable endowments of the vicars. But as the vicar was liable to be dismissed at any moment by the appropriator, he was not likely to insist too rigidly on the legal sufficiency of his stipend, and so the wretched salary was continued. Richard II.'s Statute had not the desired effect as regards the vicar's salary, and I presume a similar effect in reference to the relief of the poor.

The mistake which Richard's Parliament made was in leaving the arrangements to be carried out by the bishops, instead of the Legislature laying down distinct rules. This we find was done in 1403, eleven years afterwards (4 Henry IV. c. 12), when it was enacted that, "In every church so appropriated, a secular person be ordained vicar perpetual, canonically institute and induct in the same, and conveniently endowed by the discretion of the ordinary (1) to do divine service, (2) to inform the people, and (3) to keep hospitality there, and that none of the religiosi [monks or friars] be made vicars in any church so appropriated."

It may appear strange to learn that a remnant of this system still exists in our days. The bishops, chapters, universities, colleges, schools, charities, hospitals, and Ecclesiastical Commissioners who possess the rectorial tithes, give but a small part of them to the vicars who are performing all the parochial duties. The pernicious system of the monks is thus perpetuated. The reports of the Ecclesiastical Commission of Inquiry in 1835 disclosed a frightful state of neglect and waste of church revenues, which the Ecclesiastical Commissioners appointed in 1836, have during the past fifty years, strenuously endeavoured to rectify, and to improve their distribution. But the Commissioners cannot disturb the existing law as regards the rectorial tithes held by laymen and lay-women, colleges, schools, &c., who are not connected with the parishes from which they receive the tithes. The parochial clergy receive a little more than half of all the tithe-rent charges of the country.

The vicar perpetual of Henry IV.'s Act must not be confounded with the later title, "perpetual curate." There is this remarkable distinction between them. The former is endowed with the vicarial tithes. The latter is appointed by the appropriator, or impropriator, without any endowment from tithes, so that in such cases the rectorial and vicarial tithes, as well as landed or other endowments, have been taken away from the parish.

By the Statutes of 1392 and 1403 the vicar received a portion of the glebe lands belonging to the living and the "small" tithe which the appropriator found most difficult to collect. The rector himself—one of the bodies stated above—received, as he or she does at the present day, the "great" tithes. The most important part of Henry's Act is in giving the vicar a permanent position in the parish during his life. But the freehold tenure for life has been grossly abused. The abuses have much decreased in certain directions within the past fifty years, not by any wish on the part of many of the holders, but by the force of public opinion, and by the vigilance of Nonconformists not only in preaching the Gospel themselves, but by exposing and bringing to light the many and various abuses which flow from the freehold tenure of incumbents of the church. The most dangerous and alarming abuses of the clerical freeholder, called by some the parochial autocrat, has occurred within the past fifty years. I mean the so-called "Catholic Revival" within the Church of England. I have introduced this as an illustration to show how the clerical freehold tenure can be abused, and that vitally. As this topic is foreign to my subject, I shall not continue it, except to remark that the so-called "Evangelical Party" has equally abused the tenure by making the Church puritanical, by neglecting parish work, closing their churches from Sunday to Sunday, by living in a state of torpor and indifference to all spiritual work in their parishes. If incumbents had some parochial councils to control them, the freehold tenure would not be so abused. But in the absence of any parochial check, the incumbent is absolute within his parochial limits. This is the weakest point in the parochial system. The tenure should be limited to five years, like staff appointments in the army, then he should seek re-election or seek another sphere of labour elsewhere.

It is estimated that at the time of the Reformation there were about eight thousand five hundred parishes in England and Wales, and therefore the same number of rectors. Of this number about three thousand five hundred were appropriated with their tithes and churches to monastic, episcopal, capitular, and collegiate corporations. These corporations then became the rectors, and received the tithes and other emoluments of the parishes. In such appropriations the rectorial tithes were alienated from church purposes within the parishes. The system, as I stated, commenced with the monks, and is still perpetuated within the church. As the corporations could not discharge the religious functions of the parishes of which they were rectors, and from which they received the rectorial or "great" tithes, they appointed deputies, called "vicars," to reside in the parishes and to do the parochial duties for them. There were about five thousand parishes which were not thus annexed. The old vicars before the Reformation must not be confounded with the modern vicars. There were three classes of incumbents, viz., the rector, vicar, and perpetual curate. A large number of new rectories, vicarages, and perpetual curacies have come into existence since the Reformation, and especially since 1818, when the Church Building Society was formed. The number of benefices in England and Wales in 1831 was 10,540. Since then about 3200 have been formed, so that in 1887 the number may be taken as 13,740. Therefore, since the Reformation 5240 new benefices have been created. 13,824 incumbents and 5795 curates are now actively employed in the work of these parishes. In round numbers we may take 20,000 as the total number of working parochial clergy in A.D. 1887.

By a recent Act of Parliament, perpetual curates are entitled to be called "vicars," and many incumbents of district churches are, by recent Acts of Parliament, called "rectors;" for example, the 101 district incumbents appointed under the Parish of Manchester Act of 1850 are all called "rectors."

I now return to the history of tithes. Alexander III., who was pope from 1159 to 1181, was very active in writing to archbishops and bishops of foreign churches, commanding them to order the people to pay tithes. In 1170 he wrote to the Archbishop of Canterbury and to the Bishop of Winchester on the subject. The former prelate held a Provincial Synod in 1175 at Westminster, at which were present King Henry II., his crowned son, and all the bishops and abbots of the province. At this synod the pope's letter for the payment of tithes was read. In compliance with such orders, the synod commanded all tithes to be paid on crops from the ground and from trees, of young animals, of wool, lambs, butter, cheese, &c. Curses and excommunications were hurled against all and everyone who would not pay the tithes.

The Archbishop of York, twenty years after (1195), held a similar synod in his province, which also commanded the payment of tithes; and this synod, like that of Westminster in 1175, wound up its business with curses and excommunications—the great bug-bear of those days—against all who would not pay tithes. These archbishops were only acting up to orders from Rome. They were tools in the hands of the popes to carry out their instructions, that is, of a foreign bishop who usurped supremacy over all other Christian churches.

It is very remarkable that in the Domesday

Survey of 1086, very few references are made to tithes among the church revenues. Why is this? An answer, which I do not endorse, is given in the "National Church," vol. vii. p. 174, for 1878, thus, "Domesday Book is a survey of landed taxable property, not of mere income, and this is why tithes are not mentioned in it." It is important to note that the appropriation of tithes to monasteries is limited to the period between 1066 and 1215. Up to the time of the Conquest, laymen did not appropriate tithes to monasteries. We find in the deeds of grants, lands and churches. In the survey there were 1700 parish churches and chapels, and 995 priests. The population was then about one million and a quarter. There is no record in the survey of any tithes having been paid to churches in the following six counties, viz., Middlesex, Cornwall, Devonshire, Somersetshire, Hertfordshire, and Leicestershire. There is no record of any parish churches in the following three counties, viz., Bedfordshire, Bucks, and Surrey, and but one in Worcestershire. The tithes must have been given to the monasteries or some other ecclesiastical bodies.

CHAPTER VI.

FROM A.D. 1215 TO THE DISSOLUTION OF MONASTERIES.

THE most important canon of the English canon law for the payment of tithes, was that passed in 1295 (23 Edward I.), at a Provincial Synod held in London by Archbishop Winchelsey, who was consecrated 1294, died 1313. The canon sets forth, that on account of the various quarrels, contentions, and scandal arising between rectors and their parishioners, as regards several customs then in use of paying tithes, some uniform claim was necessary to be set forth. It then orders that tithes were to be paid on the gross value of all crops from the ground, from trees, herbs, and hay. It also sets forth how tithes were to be paid on the produce of animals, lambs, and wool. If sheep were fed in one place in winter and in a different place in summer, the tithe was to be divided. Similarly, if any one should buy or sell sheep in the middle of the time, and it was known from which parish they came, the tithe of these sheep must be divided, as it followed the two residences. But if it were not known, then that church should have the whole tithe within whose limits at the time of shearing they were found. It further states how milk was to be tithed, and that tithes were to be paid for the pasture of animals, according to their number and the number of days. Tithes were to be paid on mills, fisheries, bees, &c., &c., which were yearly renewed. There was nothing in this canon about paying tithe on timber wood, because it was part of the inheritance of the land.

The canon then passed from predial to personal tithes. Artificers and merchants were to pay tithes of the profits of their business, and carpenters, blacksmiths, weavers, and all other workmen working for wages, were to pay tithes of their wages. This meant, that after deducting all reasonable and necessary expenses, they were to pay the tenth part of the profits.

The rector was also to receive his mortuary fees, viz., the clothes worn by the person before dying, also a horse and cow. These fees were to be paid as a satisfaction to the Church for the personal tithes which he had forgotten or wilfully neglected to pay in his life-time. Henry VIII.

fixed a money payment in lieu of the mortuary fees. This was the origin of burial fees. If parishioners would not pay their tithes, they were to be excluded from the Church until they did, and if they continued contumacious, other ecclesiastical censures would follow.

In 1344 a canon was passed at a Provincial Synod of Canterbury, held at St Paul's, London, that all kind of timber wood was tithable. This canon led to bitter strife, because wood had not been previously tithable, for, like mines and quarries, it was part of the inheritance of the land. Timber wood was not tithable in the important canon of 1295.

In reference to making canons at synodical meetings, it was both profitable and pleasant work for ecclesiastics. The laymen who had to pay, were not permitted to express an opinion in the matter. The tithe system was a very elastic band. It was stretched as population and agriculture increased. We have the principle of development exhibited in a remarkable degree in the tithe question. As the power and influence of the bishops of Rome increased in the dark and middle ages, so did tithes. Yet we are told that tithes were the voluntary offerings of private individuals. I admit this to a limited extent. The question is,

Did all the landowners voluntarily grant tithes of the produce of their lands to the rectors of parishes? The synodical meetings to which I have referred prove that they were not given voluntarily, but were arbitrarily exacted by the anathemas of the Church.

Things became tithable, according to the last-quoted canon, which were not thought of in the days of Kings Offa and Ethelwulph. Provincial synodical canons of the dark and middle ages had a pretended binding force upon the people. But those ecclesiastics had just put the last straw upon the donkey's (people's) back in their synod of 1344. The young British House of Commons, then only seventy-nine years old, was roused to opposition. In 1345, 1347, and 1352, the House petitioned King Edward III. against the canon of 1344, but the petitions led to no satisfactory result. However, the Commons succeeded in 1372 in limiting the power of the canon. It was enacted (45 Edward III.) that trees of twenty years' growth and upwards should not be tithable, and that if a suit should be commenced in any spiritual court for the payment of such tithes, a prohibition should issue. This was the first victory gained as regards tithes by the House of Commons. The failures of 1345, 1347, and 1352 were caused by ecclesiastical

From 1215 to Dissolution of Monasteries. 67

influence exercised over the king. There have been previous Acts on Church questions, such as the Mortmain Act of 1297, which was a much bolder step than that of 1372, but it was rather the production of King Edward I. himself than any action of the House of Commons, owing to the nervous state of feeling among the lay nobility to check the alienation of property to the monasteries which deprived the king of help towards the defence of the country. The nobility were also becoming extremely jealous of the growing power and the luxurious living of the monastic bodies, and also of the Church dignitaries.

The Statute of Mortmain had forbidden the subjects from bequeathing lands and tenements to the religiosi without the king's licence. But it was eluded by licences of alienation. Here we have another instance of ecclesiastical ingenuity in devising plans to evade the law. Testators left property in perpetuity to support priests to pray for their souls. Hence originated thousands of chantries, which afterwards followed the same fate as the monasteries. A large proportion of landed property had thus indirectly passed into the hands of the Church. This went on until 1531, when an Act was passed that all such wills were not to hold good for more than twenty years. The Legislature very wisely thought that twenty years' prayers were quite sufficient to get a testator's soul out of purgatory.

The House of Commons was not a century old when it brought in a bill, "That no statute or ordinance of the clergy be granted without the assent of the Commons, and that the Commons be not subjected to any constitutions *which the clergy make for their own advantage*, without the assent of the Commons, for the clergy do not wish to be subjected to any statute or ordinances made by the Commons without the consent of the clergy" (Selden, pp. 228-238).

From the angry tone of the Commons on the canon of 1344, may we not naturally infer that if the House existed in 1175 or 1195 when canons were passed for the payment of tithes, or was a little older in 1295 when the most important canon was made, that "They would not be subjected to any canons which the clergy made for their own advantage without the assent of the Commons?"

In the "Englishman's Brief for his National Church," to which I have before referred, it is asked (Q. 21), "Is it not hard on the cultivators of land that they should have to pay tithes on its produce?" The answer is, that there is really no hardship in the matter. "If a person rents land which in every respect is tithe free, he pays so much more rent for it; if it be subject to tithes he pays so much less. In any case he pays the same amount, &c." May not the same argument be applied to manufactured goods, houses, &c.? Why are personal tithes not now paid? There is a supposed Scriptural authority for their payment. Why should the whole burden of paying tithes fall upon land?

It is stated in the "Brief" that the payment of tithes is as lawful and should be paid as regularly as rents, rates, and taxes. There is this very marked difference between the two payments. There is a *quid pro quo* for rents, rates, and taxes. But in many cases there is none for tithes. The tax is most objectionable and even scandalous when paid to lay impropriators, rich colleges, and schools. Even the one-fourth of the total of the tithe rent charge which they receive would give some local relief to poor struggling farmers in the reduction of their rates and taxes, or paying school fees for their children. It is a fact that the above tithe owners never contribute a shilling towards the parishes from which they draw so large a revenue. Then there is that large extent of abbey lands which is completely free from tithes, and which enables the landowners to obtain a much higher rent than those whose lands are tithable.

The Earl of Selborne makes the following remarks in his pamphlet entitled, "The Endowments and Establishment of the Church of England":—"The rectorial tithes of Selborne which belong to a college at Oxford [alienated priory property given to Magdalene by Henry VI.] were, in 1882, £447; the vicarial tithes, which alone belong of right to the Vicar of Selborne, were £336. The rectorial or lay tithes of two parishes in Basingstoke, also belonging to a college or colleges at Oxford, were in the same year £1617. A lady received the rectorial tithes of Bishop's Sutton, amounting to £1431, and one of the London companies, those of Chertsey, amounting to £1112." This is but a sample of the distribution of tithe rent charge. If we could but get a statement like the above to cover all the ground, it would open the eyes of the public as to the distribution and the recipients of the tithe rent charge outside of the parochial clergy.

In the "Brief" it is asked (Q. 28), "Were not many of the endowments which the Church of England now holds, given to the Church of Rome?" No, is the answer, and adds, "Not a single endowment was given to the Church of Rome." Both question and answer are misleading. The Church of England was never the Church of Rome. The

From 1215 to Dissolution of Monasteries. 71

correct way to put the question, but which would not suit the editor of the "Brief," is, Were not many of the endowments, which the Church of England now holds, given to her when she held the same doctrines as the Church of Rome? Yes. The main object of the grants and endowments of lands, churches, tithes, &c., was that perpetual prayers should be offered up by the recipients and their successors for the souls of the benefactors, their families, and relatives. The benefactors believed in the doctrine of purgatory, and in the efficacy of prayers to bring their souls out of it. The Church of England in pre-Reformation days believed and taught the same lucrative doctrine. She also taught that works of charity and not faith were stepping stones to heaven. If two churches, A and B, held the same doctrines, and B received large endowments in tithes, lands, &c., in support of such doctrines. Centuries afterwards B repudiates the doctrines by the teaching of which she had obtained the endowments, but still keeps them. Is it honest under such circumstances to keep the endowments? Certainly not. But it is urged, "All these endowments have been swept away, and confiscated to the Crown" ("Brief," p. 52). This is not quite true, for a large part of the lands and tithes belonging to the alien priories are now enjoyed by some of our wealthy colleges and public schools. Add to this the fact that Henry VIII. endowed out of the confiscated monastic property six bishoprics and capitular chapters, of which five exist at the present day. These facts are carefully kept out of the "Brief," and the readers are led to believe that *all the monastic endowments* were confiscated, and nothing was given back to the Church. Again, Christ Church, Oxford, the aristocratic college for the sons of our nobility, was built and endowed out of the property of the forty monasteries confiscated by Wolsey. This is one of the richest colleges in Oxford, if not the richest. Again, the eight conventual chapters, when changed, were left in possession of almost all their monastic endowments.

A large part of the episcopal and capitular endowments were originally monastic property. The year 1836 was a turning point in all these endowments. The 6 and 7 Will. IV., c. 77, created the Ecclesiastical Commission. The Commissioners utilised these endowments for the purpose of augmenting the incomes of the parochial clergy. The incumbents received up to 1885, £739,000 per annum in perpetuity towards the augmentation of their incomes. Add to this the enormous sums spent on parsonages and the erection of new churches. The average net income of the "Common Fund" is more than one million a year. *A large part* of these funds has come from what were originally monastic endowments, which were given by benefactors for *specific purposes* stated in their "trust deeds," which may be read in the "Monasticon." So some thousands of incumbents are at the present day in receipt of augmentations from the "Common Fund" to their yearly stipends from some lands originally monastic, and from some cathedral property which was given to the cathedral bodies when the Church of England had the pope as its spiritual head, and when it held exactly the same doctrines as the Church of Rome.

The duties performed by the parochial priests for the tithes were their regular duties, including (1) saying mass, (2) praying for the dead, and (3) invoking the saints. But the mass has been suppressed, the dead are not prayed for, and the saints are no longer invoked by those who now enjoy the tithe rent charge. It is stated in the "Brief," that "When the principal parochial endowments were given, papal supremacy was not admitted by the Church of England, and Roman doctrines were not held." If by "Roman doctrines" is meant the innovations introduced into the Roman Church by the Creed of Pope Pius V., founded upon the Council of Trent, then the "Brief" is correct. But this is not, I think, what the "Brief" means. I shall explain how the "Brief" is wrong in the above quotation. The endowments were not all given at once but were gradually added for about 800 years. The parochial endowments commenced on a small scale in the latter part of the seventh century, and increased in the eighth and ninth. But these were not tithes, but consisted of church, parsonage, and glebe. In the middle of the ninth century, when the pope had undoubtedly exercised power over the Church of England, tithes were given as free-will offerings on a small scale; they increased, and so did the pope's power over the English Church, in the tenth and up to the middle of the eleventh century. The Norman Conquest, in 1066, made a change. The Norman monks who looked on the pope and obeyed him as the supreme head on earth of the Christian religion, introduced a new plan by inducing landowners to appropriate churches, and lands, and tithes to them. To give an idea of the enormous impetus which had been given to the erection of monasteries from 1066 to 1215, or 149 years, there were 427 monasteries erected in England, with extensive endowments of lands and tithes. I have selected 1215, for, by the

From 1215 to Dissolution of Monasteries. 75

Council of Lateran, tithes were henceforth to be paid to the parochial clergy, thus abolishing from 1215 all appropriation of tithes from parishes. At the Conquest, there were only about 100 monasteries in the land. In 1215 there were about 527. The decadence of building and endowing monasteries commenced with the reign of Richard I. (1189). Tithes were not given to monasteries until after 1066. From 1066 to 1215 the monasteries had received the tithes of some thousands of parishes. Of course, they put vicars in the parishes to do the duties, and allowed them certain stipends. The question now is, In what respects did the Church of England differ in doctrine and discipline from the Church of Rome from the eighth to the thirteenth century, and from the thirteenth to the sixteenth century? The parochial system continued in course of formation for 500 years, viz., from A.D. 700 to A.D. 1200. During these 500 years the Church received "the principal parochial endowments." It cannot be stated with truth that "Roman doctrines were not held by the Church of England" during these 500 years. Neither can it be said in truth "that papal supremacy was not admitted" into the Church of England, during the same period.

There is no doubt whatever that the tithes would never have been given by the original donors to a church whose ministers not only ignore but utterly detest the mass, praying for the dead, and invoking the saints. To support this statement, I shall give a quotation from a speech delivered in the House of Lords by Archbishop Howley in 1840, when speaking on the Cathedral Bill. " They must consider," he says, " in what times many of the donations of property were made. The persons who had made them might, and probably would, if living in the present day, wish to see them applied in a very different manner." These remarks were made in reply to the following observations delivered in the same debate by Dr Sumner, Bishop of Winchester. " What right," he asked, " had the Legislature so to deal with property given for *certain specific purposes*, not by the State, but by individuals for ever?" The archbishop pointedly stated, in the speech quoted above, that the " certain specific purposes" existed no longer. [" Hansard's Debates, House of Lords," 1840.]

Again it is stated in the " Brief" that tithes are not endowments (!) and that they were given " without any specific condition being attached to their payment." Is it reasonable to think that tithes were given to the parish priest without a " quid pro quo "? Is not the " quid pro quo " implied in his office? The " Brief" further observes,

p. 52, "It is an interesting work for all zealous people concerned in such matters to see, as a matter of public trust, that those who now possess such property [the confiscated monastic property] shall fulfil the conditions attached to its original grant or bequest." I cannot defend for one moment the enrichment of the nobility and gentry of this country with church spoliation. But I ask myself the question, Do the Bishops of Chester, Gloucester, Bristol, Oxford, Peterborough, and their respective cathedral chapters, "fulfil the conditions attached to the original grant or bequest of the property which they possess?" We must not forget that the king who endowed the above bishoprics and chapters passed the Act commonly called "The Whip with its Six Strings;" and, further, that he died in the full belief of the doctrines of the Church of Rome, then taught in the Church of England, of which he was the supreme head.

The distinction between "Jus Parochiale" and "Jus Commune."

The former was the right of having the cure of souls and the offerings and oblations of the parishioners, but without any right to tithes. There may be "jus parochiale cum decimis."

The latter, or "jus commune," originated in free-will offerings. The tithes were first given by custom and as a free gift by any person who wished. From a custom on the part of some, it became a common right as regards all. The canon law gave the rector this common right to the tithes of his parish. But no secular law of England gave him the right. (Selden, pp. 361, 362.)

There were large tracts of lands throughout the country which were extra parochial. Who were to get the tithes of them? The canon law answered, the bishops, because they were entitled to the tithes of lands within the limits of their dioceses which were not assigned to any parish. This law would include the king's demesnes and forests. The following is a case of sharp practice on the part of bishops acting up to the canon law. It is well known that the Anglo-Saxon kings had endowed many monasteries with extensive lands, a good deal of which were waste lands. At great expense and labour the monks brought the lands to a productive state of cultivation. Then the bishops stepped in and claimed by canon law the tithes from the lands upon which they did not expend one shilling. But by common law, which overruled canon law, the kings of England alone had had the arbitrary disposition of the tithes

From 1215 *to Dissolution of Monasteries.* 79

of these lands (Selden, pp. 365-368), *e.g.*, King Edward I. granted by his charter in 1294 to the Cathedral Church of Carlisle, the tithes of certain lands and places within the royal forest of Englewood which were extra parochial. The king in his forests may build towns and churches, and confer such churches with the tithes thereof on whom he pleased. (Philimore, p. 1487.)

CHAPTER VII.

MONASTERIES.

In giving a history of tithes, it is absolutely necessary to give a brief sketch of the monasteries and monastic property in England.

Immediately after Augustin came to England, the age of building monasteries commenced. Before his arrival there were but a few monastic establishments in the island, not of the Benedictine order. The first British monastery, properly so called, was established at Glastonbury by St Patrick about A.D. 433. Previous to his arrival there was a sort of hermitage there, but when he came, he formed the hermits into a society, framed monastic rules for their guidance, and made himself their abbot.

A monastery was a place where people of both sexes lived alone, secluded from the common employment of the world for sacred studies and devotion. The British monks and nuns married until the Benedictine rule was rigidly enforced by King Edgar and Archbishop Dunstan in the tenth

Monasteries.

century. The religious houses may be classified thus—cathedral churches, abbeys, and priories. There were four chief officers in the abbeys and priories—(1) the chamberlain, who provided the monks' clothing; (2) the cellarer catered for them; (3) the treasurer or bursar collected their rents and other revenue, and paid all their expenses; (4) the sacrista or sexton took charge of the buildings and church, and all the utensils, books, pictures, &c., in them.

The Benedictine monks were originally laymen, working in a very praiseworthy manner with their hands to support themselves. Some were ordained as the needs of the monastery required, and, although ordained, they were still monks, and resided within the walls of their convent.

A glance at the names in the "Monasticon" of the founders of monasteries in the seventh century will show what a hold the monastic life had taken at that early period upon the Anglo-Saxon kings and nobles. But we must look to the Norman Period, for the full development of monastic institutes in this country. The mode of life and dress of the monks, fascinated and struck the Anglo-Saxons with awe. All these monasteries were richly endowed with extensive estates. They also monopolised the rich mortuary fees. The treasures of the Anglo-Saxon kings, of their families, and wealthy laymen, were poured into the monasteries. But the time was fast approaching when all those costly buildings, rich treasures, and priceless libraries were to be swept away and destroyed by foreign savage hordes. The Danes made their first appearance in England A.D. 787. They were implacable enemies of the Christian religion. Between 858 and 878 they rifled and burnt the British monasteries. Plunder was always their game, and therefore they first attacked the monasteries because they were defenceless, and contained immense wealth. This vandalism was disastrous to the nation, because it dried up the only channel of learning and education in the land, and destroyed the only existing libraries. The monasteries were the treasure-houses of charters and privileges granted by kings to nobles from time to time, and which were deposited for safety in those sanctuaries. A carefully-written history of the country was also kept in many of the monastic libraries. The destruction of the monasteries by the Danes, and the dispersion of their inmates among the villages, gave a powerful impetus to the erection of more parish churches; for, after the departure of the Vandals, it was much cheaper to build a wooden church than to rebuild a monastery. The monastic churches served, up to the time of their

Monasteries.

destruction, as the parochial churches in many places. When these were destroyed, the nobility, wealthy landowners, and bishops exerted themselves to supply not only the deficiencies, but to increase the number of parish churches. The inmates of the monasteries scattered through the villages took, no doubt, an active part in church-building.

The monasteries remained in ruins until the reign of King Edgar, who was a great supporter of the Church, and seemed to be under the complete control of Archbishop Dunstan—the first Episcopal pluralist—the originator of a practice, contrary to the primitive custom of the Church, which, in subsequent centuries, after Dunstan's time, was carried to a most scandalous extent. Wolsey, in more modern times, held several bishoprics at the same time, and yet one of his great objects was to reform the Church. But he should have commenced at home. At the time of the Church Reform Act of 1836, fourteen out of the twenty-seven bishops (including Sodor and Man) received £40,000 a year from *commendams*, a practice which then gave as much offence as the old system of heaping several bishoprics on one man.

The ostensible reason assigned in Dunstan's time for Episcopal pluralities was, that there was a dearth of suitable men for the appointments, but the real cause was, as in the case of Bishop Oswald, to carry out the scheme of removing the seculars, and bringing the monks into the cathedral churches.

The leading church ideas of King Edgar during his reign were (1) to rebuild the monasteries which lay in ruins, and (2) to drive the married clergy out of the convents, replacing them by monks. Dunstan, Athelwold of Winchester, and Oswald of Worcester (afterwards of York) were the king's chief agents in carrying out his schemes. It does not appear that any of the other bishops had taken a share in the work. Before King Edgar's reign the monasteries were filled with secular clergymen, who did spiritual duties outside their monasteries.

The English monks passed through three reformations. (1.) At the Council of Cloveshoe, A.D. 747, where no reference was made to Benedict's rule, although it had been framed in 529, and approved of by the Pope in 595. (2.) At the Council of Winchester, A.D. 965, where Benedict's rule was prominently set forth for general adoption. The monks were henceforth to confine themselves to their cloisters, to have no parochial cure of souls, and to adopt celibacy. These facts alone prove that the discipline of the Roman Church on the Continent was imported into the English

Monasteries.

Church long before the Norman Conquest. Some writers, in treating of tithes and church endowments, strive to show that the Church of England, before the Norman Conquest, had not the same doctrines and discipline as the Roman Church. The object of this line of erroneous argument is to show, that the endowments of the Church of England were given to her, when her doctrines and discipline were different to those of the Roman Church. The system of development was going on in the Roman Church on the Continent, and then introduced and adopted in the Church of England by her hierarchy and priests. (3.) At the Council of London, 1075, where the monks were enjoined to adhere more strictly to the rule of Benedict.

As I have stated above, before King Edgar's reign the monasteries were convents of secular married clergy, whose children kept up a monopoly of all the valuable appointments in the establishments. The result was certainly most pernicious to church and people. The clergy grew more and more indolent and illiterate, and their thoughts were entirely absorbed in the worldly affairs of their families, to the neglect of their spiritual duties. Although the monks had many faults, yet the English nation owes them a large debt of gratitude. They were better educated than the secular clergy, more refined, and therefore better able to raise the standard of civilisation in the country. That is what the married canons could not have done. The monasteries were the only schools where the children of the kings, nobility, and gentry could be educated. King Edward the Confessor received his early training in the monastery of Ely. Their schools formed models for our most ancient universities. The monasteries were like so many burning torches in the midst of darkness and ignorance, and were the only sources which could then supply men intellectually capable of occupying episcopal positions. Some of the noblest benefactors to the Church were bishops taken from the cloisters.

The Norman Conquest.

At the time of the Conquest, there were in England about one hundred monasteries and cathedral churches, possessing about one-twelfth of the land. Great changes had taken place in reference to the chief appointments in the churches and monasteries. There were nineteen bishoprics in England and Wales exclusive of the Isle of Man. Most of the Saxon bishops and abbots were replaced by Normans. The change was good. Some writers censure the Norman rulers for the change. A better educated and more refined class of men took their

Monasteries. 87

places. A careful study of their lives and acts, as recorded in the "Monasticon," will corroborate my statement.

All the property given to the religious houses in Anglo-Saxon times was held in common. But the new Norman bishops changed this arrangement in the cathedral churches. They assigned what revenues they thought fit to the canons as a common fund, and kept the rest of the church lands for their own personal use. These bishops had also initiated another innovation in the distribution of the cathedral revenues which existed until 1840. They gave separate endowments of lands or tithes or both to the deans, priors, and other principal officers of the cathedral churches for their own personal use, and separate from the common fund, of which they also had their shares. Some of the Norman bishops purchased landed estates out of their episcopal revenues, which they divided into prebends, with which they endowed prebendaries. The prebendal endowments ceased to be formed about the thirteenth century. The Cathedral Act of 1840 had taken away these separate endowments for the benefit of the common fund managed by the Ecclesiastical Commissioners.

At the time of the Conquest, the nineteen Cathedral bodies were composed of secular canons, except two, viz., Winchester and Worcester, which were composed of Benedictine monks. These two were subsequently increased to eight, viz., Canterbury, Durham, Carlisle, Ely, Norwich, and Rochester, and they so continued until the Dissolution, when they were formed into secular chapters by changing the priors into deans, and the chapters into canons. The fact that there were only two conventual chapters at the Conquest, indicates that the seculars more than held their own in face of the powerful patronage and protection of King Edgar and Archbishop Dunstan. It is doubtful whether this had been an improvement. The ranks, as I have stated, of the episcopal order were generally recruited from the monks, because competent men could not be found elsewhere. The magnificent and artistic cathedrals of this country had been designed and built by men connected with the monkish order. There is Durham, by William de Carilepho, formerly a Norman Abbot; Ely, by its last abbots; Gloucester, by its abbots; Rochester, by Bishop Gundulf, a monk; Winchester was commenced to be rebuilt by Bishop Wacelin in 1070, and was finished by William of Wickham; Bishop Wolstan laid the foundation of Worcester Cathedral Church in 1084, &c.

Monasteries.

In 1066 there were about 100 monasteries in England. From 1066 to 1215 there were 427 built, making 527 to which laymen could appropriate their tithes. In addition to these there were the foreign monasteries. The main object of granting tithes to monasteries, is contained in the usual words of the charters, "Do et concedo decimam pro anima patris mei et matris meae et pro me et uxore mea, et fratris mei, &c."

The following table of monasteries, taken from Bishop Tanner's "*Notitia Monastica*," published in 1695, will give an idea of the powerful impetus which the Norman Conquest had given to their erection in this country.

	Benedictines.	Austin Order.	Cluniacs.	Cistercians.	Colleges.	Preceptories.	Alien Priories.	Premonstratensians.	Gilbertines.	Carthusians.	Brigettan Order.	Total.
William I.,	16	6	6	...	...	...	14	...	...	...	...	42
William II.,	7	2	4	...	...	...	9	...	...	...	...	22
Henry I., .	30	40	5	10	4	2	13	...	...	...	...	104
Stephen, .	15	25	4	35	1	2	3	6	6	...	...	97
Henry II., .	22	30	6	20	3	6	8	8	4	1	...	108
Richard I.,	6	4	...	1	...	...	1	4	2	...	...	18
John, . .	7	11	...	7	...	1	2	2	6	...	...	36
Henry III.,	4	15	1	9	...	...	1	1	1	...	...	32
Edward I., .	3	2	...	3	9	1	...	...	1	...	...	19
Edward II.,	2	2	...	...	...	...	...	...	...	...	...	4
Edward III.,	3	6	...	1	17	...	...	...	...	...	...	27
Richard II.,	...	...	...	...	...	...	...	...	...	...	...	...
Henry IV.,	...	...	...	...	4	...	...	...	...	1	...	5
Henry V., .	...	1	...	...	6	...	...	...	...	1	1	9
Henry VI.,	...	...	...	...	8	...	...	...	...	...	...	8
	115	144	26	86	52	12	51	21	20	3	1	531

The governing bodies of the foreign monasteries to which landed estates, tenements, tithes, &c., in England were granted, had built priories in convenient parts of this country, and sent monks from their own monasteries to occupy them. The principal duties of these monks were to collect the rents and tithes, and transmit them to the heads of houses. It is stated that not less than £2000 a year, a sum equal to £60,000 of our money, was forwarded, in the reign of King Edward III., to Cluni in France by the Cluniac houses in England. In the wars with France King Edward I. was the first to put a stop to the transmission of money, and his successors dissolved the alien priories.

Owing to the pomp and luxuries of the hierarchy and monastic bodies, a religious revolutionary wave passed over this country in the thirteenth century. The chief landmarks were (1) the Lateran Council in 1215, (2) the appearance in England in 1217 of the Dominican, and in 1224 of the Franciscan preaching friars, (3) the Mortmain Act of 1279. The religious mania for building and endowing monasteries commenced to decline in Edward I.'s reign. [See table of monasteries, at p. 89.] The Franciscan order was founded in 1208, and the Dominican in 1215. Pope Innocent III. approved of both orders in 1215. The ruling idea of these mendicant friars was the elevation of poverty into

Monasteries.   91

a virtue; but, strange to say, that before they were in existence many years, they became the richest orders in Christendom. Wherever they were located they became the strongest supporters of the papacy, and for two hundred years, members of these orders occupied the papal throne.

The friars in England, by their powerful and zealous preaching, had become very popular, to the great loss of the parochial clergy who were steeped in ignorance and indolency. In their sermons and pamphlets, the friars strongly advised the people to pay no tithes to the parsons; that tithes were but alms and may be given to any charitable use, and that the parsons had no parochial rights to them. The result was that the people gave the tithes to the friars, both personal and predial, as alms. The parish priests seriously felt the diminution of their revenues. Convocation of course moved vigorously in the matter. The Council of Vienna, held in 1340, condemned the friars for receiving the tithes (Selden, p. 166). The begging friars knew how to draw water to their own fountain, and succeeded well. But "Holy Church" proved too powerful for them. They were pronounced "heretics" for preaching against the payment of tithes to the parsons.

John Wickliffe, Rector of Lutterworth, who died

A.D. 1384, preached the same views about tithes as the friars did. He strongly asserted that tithes were only alms, and may be given for any religious use, or retained according to the will of the donor. The Church considered his statement as heresy, and a council of ecclesiastics condemned his opinions. The cry, "The Church in danger," was then heard, as it has often been since, whenever any changes for her improvement are suggested, or when scandals and abuses are attempted to be removed. The great beneficial reforms which were effected in the Church by the Acts of 1836, 1840, and subsequent Acts, created in these days the usual cry. Everybody now admits those changes to have been beneficial. The best evidence on this matter, are the annual reports submitted to Parliament by the Ecclesiastical Commissioners. There were grave and serious abuses in the Church in Wickliffe's days. He was as hostile to the Pope's supremacy as he was against the compulsory payment of tithes. He held that kings were superior to popes, and therefore that appeals from spiritual to temporal tribunals were just, right, and lawful. Time proved his statement on this point to be correct. He must have been a man of great boldness to question in those days the supremacy of the popes. We, living in the nineteenth century, can take a

Monasteries. 93

historical survey of the various changes and struggles which occurred as regards the popes' supremacy since Wickliffe's time. He utterly detested the monks for their luxurious and worldly habits, The parochial clergy also did not escape his lash. He preferred the good old custom of one paying one's tithes, according to one's own free-will, to good and godly men, able to preach the Gospel, and he condemned, in his complaint to King Richard II. and his Parliament, the practice of compelling people to pay tithes (Selden, p. 291).

It appears from the charters which appropriated tithes to monasteries that they were given as alms in perpetuity, and this fact fortifies the statements made by Wickliffe and the Friars. They asserted that they were by custom originally given as alms or free-will offerings without any compulsion whatsoever; and Wickliffe gives some additional information, viz., that they were given only to good and godly men who were able to preach the Gospel. What seems to have excited his feelings most was, that people were in his time compelled to pay tithes to worthless and ungodly parsons who were unable to preach the Gospel. The fact that the landowners had given their tithes for any religious use, to monks who were mostly laymen, to nuns, to the religious military orders, to foreign monasteries, and this with the full approval of kings, popes, and bishops, I say that this fact proves to demonstration that tithes were not due by divine right to the evangelical priesthood; that they were property which could have been and was disposed of, like any other kind of property, to whatever use the benefactor or owner wished. By clerical pressure at home, especially in the Confessional box, acted upon by ecclesiastical pressure from Rome, the landowners and those who paid personal tithes in this country, had slowly acquiesced in the custom, and this acquiescence created a common right in the tithes by rectors of parishes and other ecclesiastical corporations to which they were given. The usual question at Confession was, Did you pay your tithes? If No was the answer, there was no absolution granted. Protestants do not understand the extraordinary power exercised by priests in the Confessional box. To show that tithes were at first given as alms, the following extract from one of the numerous charters granting tithes to monasteries will sufficiently indicate. *supra 53.*

Charter of Earl Randulph Gernons of Chester to the Monastery of Chester.

" Universitati vestrae notum facio me dedisse in *elemosina in perpetuum* Deo et S. Mariae et eccle-

Monasteries. 95

siae S. Werburgae et Rudulpho abbati et conventui dictae ecclesiae pro salute animae Hugonis comitis, praedictae ecclesiae fundatoris ac pro salute animae Randulphi comitis patris mei, et antecessorum meorum, et pro salute animae meae, et Christianorum omnium, omnem decimam integriter et plenariè omnium reddituum meorum civitatis Cestriae, &c."—["Monasticon."]

This Earl died in 1153. Earl Hugh Lupus, the refounder, who died in 1101, granted many manors, churches, and tithes, as *alms in perpetuity*.

All the early parochial records are lost, and therefore in dealing with the old parishes we are at a great disadvantage. It is not so with the monasteries. The monastic bodies had carefully preserved all their charters of grants. That beautiful storehouse—the "Monasticon"—furnishes us with ample information for our guidance, and a correct knowledge of those houses. Is it not reasonable, in the absence of parochial records, to draw conclusions from monastic charters, as to the original disposition of tithes to parishes? If they were given as alms to monasteries, they were also so given to parochial clergy, and if so given, it is unreasonable to suppose they were given to the rectors for their own personal use without any reference to the poor and sick, or the fabric of the church. As they were orginally given as voluntary offerings, they formed a part of the parochial common fund. This fund was not for the exclusive use of the clergy. I have already stated its use.

CHAPTER VIII.

INFEUDATIONS—EXEMPTION FROM PAYING TITHES.

INFEUDATIONS are the conveyances of the perpetual right of tithes to laymen.

The Third Council of Lateran, held in 1180, was the first to forbid infeudations. Such conveyances, although frequent on the Continent, were not so in England until the general dissolution of monasteries. Very little of the lands, tenements, and tithes of the alien priories which Parliament had at various times alienated, was given away or sold to laymen. The properties were bestowed on other monasteries and colleges for religious and educational purposes. This was not so with the enormous properties which Parliament had given to Henry VIII. and his son. The 32 Hen. VIII., c. 7, gave the king power to grant the lands, tenements, tithes, &c., of the dissolved houses to whom he wished; that such persons should be free from the payment of tithes if such lands had been exempted previous to the Dissolution; and the same Statute also permitted the lay-owners of monastic lands to claim tithes from them. So, therefore, the layman who claimed the payment of tithes was called an "impropriator," because he was an "improper" person to receive them. But the same may have been said of the lay monks, nuns, military orders, &c., who had been in the receipt of tithes.

It is a well-known fact that the lay-owners of tithes never contributed any of them, before the Commutation Act, for Church purposes. They have always been, and are still, the most exacting to obtain their tithes, or tithe rent charges in full.

Exemption from Paying Tithes by Religious Houses.

All abbots, priors, and other heads of monasteries had originally paid tithes; but Pope Paschal II. exempted generally all the "religiosi" from the tax on lands under their own management. About A.D. 1160 Pope Adrian IV. limited this exemption to the Templars, Hospitallers, and Cistercians, who alone were exempted from paying tithes for lands which were then, but not those afterwards acquired, under their own immediate management. The privilege did not extend to lands let to farmers, but only to those which they occupied before the Council of Lateran, in 1215, which confirmed the above exemptions. A fourth

Infeudations.

order—the Premonstratensian—was added by Pope Innocent III. These were called the four privileged orders. After the passing of the Mortmain Act, which gave a terrible blow to the monastic bodies, the privileged orders purchased from the popes, bulls of exemption from paying tithes for their lands let to farmers, and also for the lands which they acquired since 1215. These bulls had the force of law in the English canon law, and were allowed in actions for tithes. This mode of purchasing bulls of exemption was put a stop to in 1400 by 2 Henry IV., c. 4, which subjected the purchaser to premunire (Selden, pp. 406, 407 ; Philimore, p. 493). The Statute of Premunire was passed in 1393 (16 Richard II., c. 5) against "procuring, at Rome or elsewhere, any translations, processes, excommunications, bulls, instruments, or other things which touch the king, against him, his crown and realm, and all persons aiding or assisting therein shall be put out of the king's protection, their lands and goods forfeited to the king's use, and they shall be attached by their bodies to answer to the king and his council, or process *proemunire facias* shall be made out against them, as in any other cases of provisors."

The lands of the religiosi, which were thus exempted from paying tithes, are exempted up to the present day, because at the dissolution of monasteries, before as well as during the reign of Henry VIII., the 31 Henry VIII., c. 13, provided that all lands held by the monasteries, and exempted from tithes, should also be exempted when vested in the Crown; and the king had an Act passed exempting those who should become possessors of such crown property. There is also 2 Edward VI., c. 13. But there were other lands given to the king at the dissolutions which were not exempted; in such cases the law of exemption did not apply. This explains the fact that some of the present holders of monastic property pay no tithes, some do, and others are tithe owners. Up to 1571 every man might by common law be discharged from paying tithes by grants, or compositions real; but since 13 Elizabeth, no real composition is good for any longer than three lives, or twenty-one years.

The modus and real compositions tended, like the Commutation Act of 1836, to the improvement of estates.

CHAPTER IX.

THE DISSOLUTION OF MONASTERIES.

WHAT precedents had King Henry VIII. to guide him in dissolving the monasteries?

(1.) Edward I., in 1295, seized the property of the alien priories.

(2.) In 1324 (17 Edward II.) the lands and tenements held in England by the Templars were, by Act of Parliament, seized and transferred to the Knights Hospitallers, when the services of the former were no longer required for purposes for which the property had been assigned to them.

(3.) Edward III., in 1337, seized the alien priories, and let out the lands and tenements, until there was peace with France in 1361. The most valuable of them were naturalized, and thus became free from the yoke of any foreign monastery, and could elect their own priors.

(4.) Richard II. bestowed on the Cartusians several of the smaller alien priories which Edward III. had seized.

(5.) In the reign of Henry IV. the House of

Commons suggested, in 1404, that the clergy, including the religiosi, should be deprived of all their temporalities, in order to furnish funds for the defence of the kingdom and for the maintenance of a large army. A similar proposal was made in 1410, but the king, directly influenced by the Archbishop of Canterbury, would not listen to the suggestions. These facts indicate the growing unpopularity of the Church even at that early period of the life of the House of Commons. The statute of Mortmain in 1279, the statutes of Provisors in 1351 (25 Edward III., c. 6) and of 1353 (27 Edward III.), the statute of Premunire in 1393, are all so many previous illustrations of the growing hostile feeling of Parliament to the Church, monastic establishments, and the Pope of Rome.

(6.) In the reign of Henry V. another attack was made upon the property of the Church by the Parliament which met in 1415, but the tact of the Archbishop of Canterbury on this occasion, as well as in 1404 and 1410, saved the property. However, this Parliament granted the king all the property of the alien priories, except those which were free and could elect their own priors. Henry V. built and endowed six colleges and three religious houses principally out of the property of the suppressed priories.

The Dissolution of Monasteries.

(7.) Henry VI. founded and endowed Eton College and King's College, Cambridge, out of the same suppressed property.

(8.) Cardinal Wolsey, with the approval of King Henry VIII. and the pope, suppressed about forty small religious houses in 1523, in order to endow his college—Cardinal College, now Christ Church, Oxford—one of the richest in that University.

Here are instructive and interesting facts. Large monastic endowments were devoted to building and richly endowing colleges and schools for the sons of the wealthy men of the land. Up to a recent date, a large part of the endowments of Oxford and Cambridge was given away in the shape of hundreds of superfluous Fellowships with stipends annexed ranging from £200 to £450 a year, tenable in certain cases for life. Here was a wholesale waste of endowments. The recipients left their colleges for ever, and did no work for their handsome life annuities. Men have spent thirty and forty years of their lives in the service of their sovereign through all parts of the empire who have been pensioned off with less than these men have pocketed from their Universities after a few years' study. The endowments of Oxford were so enormous that nothing but a Royal Commission could dare attempt to find out its financial position. The ex-Fellows generally went to professions, and were not handicapped in their finances like less fortunate individuals in the great struggle at the beginning of their professional career, just at a time when so many failures occur from want of funds. It seems strange that while millions of the poor are educated partly at the expense of the rates and taxes, partly by voluntary contributions, and partly by the parents themselves, yet our leading wealthy Universities and some of our public schools are in the enjoyment of rich endowments from monastic property and rectorial tithes. Add to these the facts that so many extensive estates, &c., were given by Henry VIII. to his favourites and courtiers, and that lay impropriators are at present in receipt of £766,233 a year from tithe-rent charges, minus the expenses and depreciation in value of this kind of property. In all the distribution of Church spoliation, the poor have never been considered for one moment.

I have stated eight precedents for Henry VIII.'s guidance in dissolving the monasteries. I shall now state his action in the matter.

In 1534 Parliament made him "Supreme head of the Church of England." He therefore took the pope's place, and received the first-fruits and tenths. In 1535 commissioners were appointed to

The Dissolution of Monasteries. 105

take the value of all ecclesiastical benefices in order to settle the first-fruits and tenths. In 1536 the valuation was completed. The monks viewed the king's conduct towards the pope with the most bitter hostility. They constantly used their influence to excite the feelings of the people against the king. Henry knew all this, but he could never alienate them from the pope. The subsequent conduct of the king and his ministers was guided on political and not religious grounds. There was then but one course open to the king, and that was to dissolve the religious houses. It was a bold, arduous, and dangerous step. The morality of these houses was the only vulnerable point in which he thought he could successfully carry out his plan. He first obtained an Act of Parliament empowering him "to visit, order, and reform all errors and abuses in religion." This was the lever which Henry's agents used to expose every real and imaginary immoral act, and thus create hostility in the minds of the people against them. A commission was issued in 1535 with unlimited power to visit the monasteries. In 1536 the report was finished. But the original was destroyed in Queen Mary's reign. We must be careful what credence to give to evidence taken down and reported upon by such commissioners as Leigh and Leyton, who had not scrupled to suborn witnesses. An Act was passed, 27 Henry VIII., caps. 27, 28, dissolving every monastery which had a revenue of less than £200 a year, and transferring to the king all the monasteries, priories, and other religious houses, all the sites, circuits, churches, chapels, advowsons, patronage, manors, granges, lands, hereditaments, tithes, pensions, annuities, rights, &c., which belonged to such monasteries; and that "the king shall have them in as large and ample a manner as the governors of those houses possessed them." "That he was to have and to hold them, his heirs and assigns, to do and use therewith his and their own wills, to the pleasure of God and to the honour and profit of this realm." By this Act 376 houses were dissolved. The king received £32,000 a year from the property, respecting the vested rights of leaseholders, and, in addition, he obtained plate, jewels, and personal effects to the value of £100,000. He gave small pensions to some abbots, priors, and monks; others he transferred to the larger monasteries. The houses were stripped of their lead, bells, glass, and materials, which were sold to the neighbouring gentry.

The conditions upon which all the vast monastic property was given by Parliament to the king were, "That they were to be used to the pleasure of God, and to the honour and profit of this realm." Did Henry VIII. or his successors carry out these conditions? They certainly did not. The property of the alien priories was insignificantly small as compared with the enormous property which Parliament granted to Henry VIII. But there was this distinction between them. Almost all the former property was devoted to religious and educational purposes. Laymen received little or nothing. But the case was very different with Henry VIII.'s confiscations. His courtiers and favourites, and those of Edward VI. and Elizabeth, were most eager to share and did obtain monastic estates and tithes, and episcopal and capitular properties, which many of their successors still hold —for instance, the Duke of Bedford, with £150,000 a-year from abbey lands; others sold them, and thus much of the property has been handed down to the present time through a long line of purchasers.

Henry VIII. intended to create twenty-one bishoprics, and to suitably endow them from the vast monastic properties which Parliament had given him. But only six were created and endowed. Some of Henry's courtiers and favourites who received inferior monastic lands, induced the king to make certain of his bishops and chapters exchange their good lands for the inferior lands of the courtiers and favourites, and also to exchange the impropriated tithes for an equal value of episcopal and capitular landed estates. These exchanges were very numerous in the reigns of Edward and Elizabeth. An Act was passed, 1 Eliz. c. 19, which authorised the queen to take in her hands, on the voidance of any bishopric, so much of the lands belonging to it as should be equal in value to the confiscated rectorial tithes belonging to the Crown in that diocese, and to exchange such tithes for the lands. Some of these lands were then given to her ministers and favourites, some were kept by the Crown, and others sold to furnish funds for national purposes, so as to prevent application to Parliament for money. It was in this manner that bishops and cathedral chapters lost so much landed property and came into possession of large revenues from tithes which belonged to the dissolved monasteries.

The suppression of the larger monasteries was to be carried out if possible by voluntary surrender. The commissioners tried in every way to persuade them to surrender by promising the abbots and priors good pensions during life, for no charges of immorality could have been preferred against the houses. In 1536-7 there were but three surrenders;

The Dissolution of Monasteries.

in 1537-8 there were twenty-four. The commissioners induced those who surrendered to persuade others to follow their example, for it was the king's policy to let the public see that the surrenders were freely made. When persuasion failed, the commissioners used threats. The monks of the Charterhouse were committed to Newgate, where five of them died, and five more were on the point of death from the cruel and barbarous treatment received there. Whiting, Abbot of Glastonbury, Coke, Abbot of Reading, and Beche, Abbot of St John's, Colchester, were executed. These acts drove terror into those who had not yet surrendered. In 1538-9 there were one hundred and seventy-four surrendered, and in 1539-40 there were seventy-six. In April 1539 Parliament ratified the surrenders up to that time, and allowed the king to extend the Act to all the other monasteries which had not yet surrendered. Some of the nobility were promised estates by free gifts from the king; others obtained them by easy purchase. The members of the House of Commons were also promised large shares, and of course Henry's agents dangled before the people, "No more subsidies, no fifteens, no loans, no common aids," as the wealth of the dissolved monasteries was ample to maintain an army of 40,000 men, and so to dispense with all taxation. The Church was also to be pleased. There were to be twenty-one new bishoprics, with cathedrals, deans, and chapters endowed out of the property. This number, however, was reduced to six. Westminster existed only about nine years. Five still exist. Gloucester and Bristol are united, but they are to be separated again when funds are collected to endow the Bristol bishopric.

In 1540 there were 645 of the large monasteries suppressed. In 1546, 90 colleges, 110 hospitals, 2347 chantries were handed over to the king by Parliament. The total revenue which the king received was about £200,000 a year, which, according to the present value of money, was not less than £2,000,000 per annum. To sell this property, say at 30 years' purchase, we reach a capital of £60,000,000, some estimate it at £100,000,000.

The following laws were passed for the payment of tithes :—

(1.) 27 Hen. VIII. c. 20 (1535) provides that "all tithes should be paid according to the ecclesiastical laws and ordinances of the Church of England, and after the laudable usages of the parish or place where the party dwelt."

(2.) 32 Hen. VIII. c. 7 (1540). In the 5th sec. of this Act, it is stated that no tithes are to be paid

The Dissolution of Monasteries.

for lands discharged from paying tithes, or are not chargeable in the payment of tithes.

(3.) 2 and 3 Ed. VI. c. 13. This Act had made important changes in the payment of tithes. It has been referred to in another part of this book. (See p. 132, No. 5.)

CHAPTER X.

THE COMMUTATION ACT OF 1836, 6 AND 7 WILL. IV., C. 71.

Up to the time this Act was passed, the tithe owner claimed in kind the tenth part of the gross produce of the land, without contributing anything towards cultivation or improvements. In fact the claim retarded both, and the object of the Act was to advance and not to keep back the cultivation and improvement of the land. The tithe was a tax upon labour and capital. The collection of tithes became both unpopular and obnoxious.

"Tithes are a tax," says Archdeacon Paley, "not only upon industry, but upon that industry which feeds mankind. They operate as a bounty upon pasture. The burden of the whole tax falls upon tillage, that is, upon that precise mode of cultivation which it is the business of the State to relieve and remunerate in preference to every other." [Paley's "Moral and Pol. Philosophy," vol. ii. p. 406.]

The Commutation Act of 1836.   113

"The tithe," says Adam Smith, "is always a great discouragement both to the improvements of the landlord and to the cultivation of the farmers. The one cannot venture to make the most important, which are generally the most expensive improvements, nor the other to raise the most valuable, which are generally, too, the most expensive crops, when the Church, which lays out no part of the expense, is to share so very largely in the profit." [Smith's "Wealth of Nations," vol. iii. p. 274.]

Agricultural depression during the four years previous to 1836, and the growing discontent of agricultural tithe-payers, demanded a speedy solution of this problem. Statesmen tried to solve it before Lord Russell attempted the task. Lord Althorp tried it in 1833, and again in 1834, but failed on both occasions. His three principal propositions were—(1) To substitute a money payment in lieu of tithes in kind; (2) the rent-charge to bear a fixed proportion to the rent payable on the land; (3) to redeem the tithe by twenty-five years' purchase, or the creation of a rent-charge of equal value. The second proposition was the weakest. Any attempt to establish a proportion between tithe and rent would end in failure, for the two had no similar foundation. Tithe was founded upon produce, but rent was not. Lord Althorp would make tithe to fluctuate with rent, retaining a fixed proportion of rent-charge. In principle it was a tax on capital, and therefore failed.

In 1835 Sir Robert Peel, when Prime Minister, introduced a bill on the same subject. The principle contained in his Bill was that there should be a fixed money payment in the shape of a corn rent in lieu of tithes, varying yearly according to the price of the three corns, wheat, barley, and oats; that it should be a voluntary arrangement between the tithe-owner and tithe-payer. The machinery to carry out this Bill was to appoint three commissioners, viz., two by the Crown and one by the Archbishop of Canterbury. These commissioners should appoint assistant commissioners. Within a month after he had introduced this Bill, his Government went out of office (8th April 1835).

Lord John Russell, a member of Lord Melbourne's Government which succeeded Sir R. Peel's, took up the subject of tithes, by introducing a Government Bill on the 9th February 1836. "Tithe," his lordship said, "was a discouragement to industry, a penalty on skill, a heavy mulct on those who expended the most capital and displayed the greatest skill in the cultivation of the land." These were true words, and it gives one pleasure

The Commutation Act of 1836.

to observe that he had the courage to boldly express his opinions. His boldest statement was that "Tithes were the property of the nation." This remark has again and again been quoted by the opponents of tithes, and it has as often been contradicted by the supporters of tithes.

Lord Russell rejected Lord Althorp's plan which related to the establishment of a proportion between tithe and rent. He adopted the machinery and some other parts of Sir Robert Peel's. The principles contained in Lord Russell's Bill were that the landowner or tenant might agree with the tithe-owner *to commute the tithe*, whether paid by modus or composition or otherwise, *into a corn rent payable in money and permanent in quantity, but fluctuating yearly in value*, so that in future any improved value given to land would not increase the amount of the rent charge. The corns were to be wheat, barley, and oats. The base of calculation was to be the average tithe paid for the seven years previous to Christmas 1835. The arrangement was to be voluntary up to 1st October 1838, then compulsory. The Bill at first was but tentative, and was materially changed in its progress through the House.

The Commutation Act made a great change. The tithe was no longer to be paid on the produce or *increase* of the land as stated in the Mosaic Law, and it was upon this Law the payment by Christians was founded. The Act made the tithe a direct charge on the land itself and not on its produce. Before the passing of the Act, the tithe-owner had to sue the tithe-payer in the county court for arrears, but after the passing of the Act, he can distrain on the land for arrears, and the Act empowers the tithe-owner to go on any other land belonging to the same landlord and in the same parish to recover the arrears of rent charge should the land from which the tithe was due be unable to satisfy his claim and costs. The tithe-owner has a prior claim to the landlord's, because the charge is prior to produce, therefore it is a charge prior to any rent.

The following statement will serve as an illustration of Lord Russell's Act. A money payment was fixed by the Tithe Commissioners on an average of seven years' payment of tithes. Let this be £100; the one-third of this, viz., £33, 6s. 8d., is for wheat, the same sum for barley, and the same for oats. The average prices of the three corns per bushel for the seven years previous to 1835 is—for wheat, 7s. 0¼d., for barley, 3s. 11½d., for oats, 2s. 9d. The tithe rent-payer has to pay in respect of his £100 rent charge, the price of

The Commutation Act of 1836.

94·95 bushels of wheat, 168·42 bushels of barley, and 242·42 bushels of oats. Early in January of every year a duly authorised advertisement is inserted in the *London Gazette* by order of the Comptroller of Corn, stating the average prices of wheat, barley, and oats for the seven years then next preceding. The serious objection to this plan is that the average prices of the three cereals are calculated on the prices sold to the millers, which included the cost of freight and the freights of one or more middlemen, instead of calculating on the prices sold by the farmers. This false system enhances the value of the rent charge. The tithe-payer is liable for this rent charge whether the above three cereals are grown or not, or even if the lands be uncultivated.

Supposing that for any year, say 1885, wheat was advertised in the *London Gazette* at 5s. 1¾d. per bushel, barley, 3s. 11¾d., oats, 2s. 8¼d., what has the tithe-owner to receive for £100 tithe-rent charge?

He receives (94·95 × 61¾ + 168·42 × 47¾ + 242·42 × 32¼) = £90, 10s. 3½d.

The 80th section of the Act says that "any tenant who shall pay any such rent charge shall be entitled to deduct the amount thereof from the rent payable by him to his landlord, and shall be allowed the same in account with his landlord."

There are few instances in which the tenants deduct the tithes from their rents according to this section. The general practice is that the farmer, in his lease or agreement, agrees to pay the tithes himself to the tithe owner, and the rent is computed accordingly. The rent is therefore less than it would really be when the tenant had agreed to pay the rent charge himself. It therefore follows that the tenant pays the tithes for the landlord. If a tenant should take a farm without making any such agreement, then the 80th section comes into force. The landlord, by the above lease or agreement, thus contracts himself out of this section. There is no doubt that the Legislature in 1836 intended that the landlords should pay the rent charges, and thus prevent any friction in the collection between the clergyman and his parishioners. To remove this friction, we must expect at the meeting of Parliament in 1887 that the Government will bring in a short Bill making landlords pay the rent charges.

If a tenant should agree with his landlord to pay a rental of say £500 per annum, and £100 tithe rent charge, I consider that the former is bound to pay the tithe owner his tithe rent of £90, 10s. 3½d. (1886), because he is paying only the landlord's debt. The landlord allows him the money in a

The Commutation Act of 1836.   191

reduced rental. That being so, it is dishonest on the part of the farmer not to pay the landlord's debt. Supposing the engagement was the 80th section of the Act; then the rent would be £600; the farmer pays the landlord £600 rental, and the landlord pays himself £90, 10s. 3½d. to the tithe owner. If the farmer paid the rent charge himself and received a deduction in his rent, it would be an abatement in the half-year's rent of £250. As it is, he has two abatements, viz., from the landlord, and from the tithe owner, by paying only £90, 10s. 3½d., instead of £100. But he is not satisfied with this 9½ per cent., he also *demands* 10 to 15 per cent. of an abatement out of the half-year's rent charge, or 20 to 30 per cent. on the year's charge, plus the 9½ per cent. fall in the value of the tithe rent charge for 1886. The rent charge in 1887 is but £87, 8s. 9¾d., or over 12½ per cent. below par value. In discharging the landlord's debt to the tithe owner, every candid and honest man will condemn the farmer for not carrying out his contract. The whole blame is to be attached to the Commutation Act for having created dual landlords. There should be but one landlord, and he should be compelled to pay the tithe rent charge himself out of the rent received from his tenant, and the rent of his tenant should include the tithe rent charge. The landlord would gain by the arrangement. At present, he allows his tenant £100 to pay a debt of £90, 10s. 3½d. (or £87, 8s. 9¾d. in 1887), which the tenant declines to pay, unless he receives an abatement of from 20 to 30 per cent.

But here is the anomaly of the Commutation Act, that although the rent charge comes out of the landlord's pocket, yet the tithe owner cannot by law bring an action against him for any arrears, but is bound by the Act to distrain on the land. The tenant has therefore two landlords. Hence we find in years of agricultural depression, such as the present, tenants who receive a deduction in the half-year's rents from their landlords, seek also for a similar deduction from their second landlord—the tithe owner. These applications are generally made to incumbents, who prefer making the deduction than run the odium resulting from distraints on the lands of their parishioners. Other tithe owners, such as the Ecclesiastical Commissioners and some of the colleges, by showing a determined front in making distraints on the lands, get all their rent charges without any abatement. Similar conduct was pursued before the Commutation Act was passed; the parochial clergy, in the most sympathetic manner, accepted very low tithes in years of agricultural depression. The result was that the rent charge arranged up to Christmas 1835

The Commutation Act of 1836.

for them and their successors, was comparatively low; whereas the tithe rent charges of the lay impropriators, colleges, schools, &c., who always insisted on their full tithes, were comparatively high, and it is upon that value they now receive their rent charges.

When the Commutation Bill was passing through Parliament in 1836 it was urged that many landlords were often absent from the country for a considerable time, and therefore if the rent charges were not paid, the tithe owners would find it very difficult to get them from absent landlords, who had no agents in the country. The law was therefore framed to enable the tithe owners to distrain on the land for arrears of rent charge, just in the same manner as the landlords could for arrears of rent. That was the origin of dual landlordism.

The Commutation Act enacts that the incumbent may receive 20 acres in lieu of his rent charge, and that the rent charge is liable to parliamentary, parochial, county, and other rates, charges and assessments, to which the tithes were liable.

The great injustice of tithe rent charges is that they are levied only upon agricultural produce, thus leaving free of such charges the extensive city and town lands, and the rich mines of the country. The lands in the vicinity of large cities and towns which produced a rental of £3 an acre, and tithe 10s., when converted to building purposes may produce a ground rent of £300 a year an acre, besides a reversion of the house property at the end of the lease. In such cases the tithe owner receives no tithes on the building value. Thus the value of the landlord's acre is increased one hundred fold, but the tithe is not increased, and thus the growing value of the land leaves no part of it for the support of religion. [Sir James Caird's "Landed Interest."]

When the Commutation Act was passed, there was much boasting by the supporters of the Church as to the humility of the clergy who had not petitioned Parliament, or held any meetings to protest against the Bill while passing through Parliament. There was good reason for their silent acquiescence. The Church had made a good bargain under the circumstances. The expense of collecting the tithes in kind sometimes reached 50 per cent. of the gross value. The tithe owner is now relieved of this expense and trouble, and the Act has also given him a firm security. The old style of collecting tithes, especially in bad seasons, often degraded the clergyman in the eyes of his parishioners.

Sir James Caird, in his book entitled "Landed Interest," says: "Since the passing of the Tithe

Commutation Act in 1836 to 1876, the rent of tithable land has increased from thirty-three millions a year to fifty millions a year. The tithe rent charge in 1836 was four millions, and is about the same still." He then asserts that the Church has lost two millions a year by the Act. How do matters stand in 1886? The rentals are fully 35 per cent. less than those in 1876. The rent charge is nearly 23 per cent less. The present rents are therefore about the same as in 1836. If the old principle of participation of tithes in kind had continued, the tithe owners would in 1886 be receiving not six but four millions in kind instead of £3,668,857 gross rent charge. It is now generally stated by Church defenders that the Church lost and the landlords gained two millions by the Commutation Act, quoting Sir James Caird's statement, but he refers to the rentals of 1876, and not to those ten years later (1886). Instead of two millions, the loss to the tithe owners in 1887 by agricultural depression would be about half a million in kind. But now the tithe rent charge is paid in cash and not in kind; and the expense of collection and selling in kind would probably leave but a small margin of this half million as a loss.

I think the Commutation Act had something

to do with the increase of rentals. For both landlords and tenants, before the passing of the Act, were unwilling to improve the land in order to give the profits to the clergy. The Act changed that feeling. When it is now said that if the Commutation Act had not been passed, the clergy would be in receipt of larger revenues from the tithes than they at present enjoy. I have shown above that this would not occur.

The main aim of clergymen at the present time on all financial matters, is not to be a tax-collector, not to come into direct contact with the givers and payers, but to have "buffers." For instance, the Commutation Act made the landlords the buffers between the clergy and their parishioners. The Ecclesiastical Commissioners are very large buffers in almost all church matters, and in the present agitations about the payment of rent charges, it is proposed to make the Commissioners collectors, so as to be buffers between the parson and the farmers whose landlords have contracted themselves out of the Act. But this is bound soon to be remedied by Parliament, and so will the distraint on the lands to recover arrears. Again, the churchwardens act as buffers between the incumbent and his congregation.

In order to do away with all future agitations on

tithes, it is proposed to redeem the tithe rent charge at twenty years' purchase, and invest the proceeds in 3 per cent. consols. This interest is to be called "The Clerical Fund," from which augmentations to clerical incomes are to be made. This is a large question. It is a proposal to deal with large private properties for general purposes. The first question to be asked, Is £100 consols to be given for £100 tithe rent charge? Some will say, Yes, but I say, No. The tithe owner has to pay about one-third of the £100 in certain expenses, and allowances for reduction in value. He should therefore get in 1887 only £67 for his £100 tithe rent charge. The subject of the redemption of tithe rent charges is further discussed in chapter xii.

The Extraordinary Tithe Rent Charge.

On one important point, Lord Russell had deviated in the second reading of his Bill from its leading principle. A deputation of Middlesex market-gardeners waited upon him after the Bill was introduced, and pointed out that they had expended a large amount of capital on the improvement of their market gardens for the past seven years, and if they were to pay a rent charge on the average of these seven years, they would continue liable to a very heavy charge, while the owners of arable land or common land in their neighbourhood, paying very low tithe composition, would come into competition with thēm, and thus they would be ruined. This argument had actually influenced his lordship even against his will, and so he introduced an extraordinary rent charge, calculated on each acre, in addition to the ordinary rent charge on hop grounds, orchards, and market gardens, brought into new cultivation. In introducing the Bill, and before the Middlesex market-gardeners influenced him, he used these remarkable words:—" Whatever might be done with orchards and gardens now existing, he felt considerable difficulty in rendering land that might be converted into orchards or gardens in future, liable to increase tithes. Orchards were a precarious and uncertain description of property, and frequently did not bear in certain years; and in respect of garden lands, if the legislature allowed the question to be opened again from time to time, it would give rise to incessant disputes." [Hansard's " Debates," vol. xxxi., Feb. 9, 1836.]

Although in the second reading he modified these views, yet he was thoroughly opposed to the principle. And his prophetic words, stated above, were fully realised in the subsequent amendment

The Commutation Act of 1836.

Acts which were necessary to be made as regards extraordinary rent charges.

No extraordinary charge was by the Act to be made the first year for new cultivations, and only one half the charge for the second year, but the full charge the third year. In thus deviating from the principle of his Bill, he made this remark:— "Tithes on extremely valuable crops, such as hops, orchards, and market gardens, could not be allowed to enter into an average for a general commutation." From the passing of the Act up to the present time, this extraordinary rent charge has been a fruitful source of discontent, because it is a tax on capital and labour, against which the principle of the Commutation Act was framed.

It keeps almost stationary the cultivation of hops and market gardens, instead of extending them. The hop proprietors were at the time in favour of the petition of the market gardeners. When lands should go out of cultivation of hops, or orchards, or market gardens, they would then be subject only to the ordinary rent charge. But all new cultivations were to pay the extraordinary rent charge, which in some cases reached as high as 30s. per acre. When this was added to the ordinary charge, the whole profit was absorbed, especially since the hop growers have now to compete with foreign countries which pay no tithes nor import duties.

It may be said that the duty on hops having been repealed since 1862, the reduction of about £4, 5s. per acre must have benefited the hop growers. The fact is, that the landlords and not the tenants chiefly derive the profits from the reduction. Before 1836 there were 56,300 acres of hops cultivated. In 1880 there were 66,703 acres. The Tithe Commissioner had taken certain hop districts, and ascertained the average tithe of the last seven years, and fixed the amount of the extraordinary charge.

The Market Gardens Act of 1873 was passed on account of a burst of popular indignation against the conduct of the Vicar of Gulval in Cornwall, who endeavoured to enforce the payment of an extraordinary tithe rent charge of 1s. 6d. per acre on 213 acres brought into new cultivation. It was enacted that the provisions relating to the extraordinary charge on market gardens, newly cultivated as such, *should only apply to parishes where such charge was distinguished at the time of commutation.*

In 1839 (2 and 3 Vict., c. 62, sec. 27) an Act was passed in a quiet manner which placed orchards, as regards the extraordinary charge, on the same footing as the Act of 1873 (36 and 37 Vict., c. 42) placed the market gardens. The Acts of 1839 and 1873 admit that extraordinary rent charges are wrong in principle, and that those on hops should be abolished.

The battle about extraordinary tithe rent charge which has been waged ever since Lord Russell inserted the unfortunate clause in his Commutation Act, has ceased by the passing of the Extraordinary Tithe Redemption Act of 1886. But there are rumours that the Act is so unsatisfactory that it must be repealed.

The following is a brief summary of that Act:—

The Extraordinary Tithe Redemption Act (49 *and* 50 *Vict., c.* 54).

This Act was passed in 1886 (25th June). In the preamble it is stated that the extraordinary charge levied under previous Acts, is an impediment to agriculture, and therefore should be limited, and power given to redeem the same. It is enacted that after the passing of this Act, no extraordinary charge shall be charged or levied under the Tithe Commutation Acts on any hop ground, orchard, fruit plantation, or market garden newly cultivated as such. The Land Commissioners are authorised to fix the capital value of the extraordinary charge payable on each farm or parcel of land at the date of the passing of the Act. The third section indicates the manner in which the capital value is to be ascertained. Such land is to be charged with the payment of an annual rent charge equal to four per centum on the capitalised value of the extraordinary charge, in lieu of the extraordinary charge. This rent charge shall be payable half-yearly on the days on which the extraordinary charge was made payable. Arrears of rent charge are to be recovered in one of the High Courts of Justice, or a county court, "or in the same way that rent charge in lieu of ordinary tithe is recoverable and subject to like conditions, or by entry upon and perception of the rents and profits of the land subject to such rent charge." The rent charge is not to be subject to any parochial, county, or other rate, charge, or assessment. The rent charge may be redeemed by the owner or other person interested in any land subject to an extraordinary charge, or rent charge substituted therefor. The redemption money to be paid to the Governors of Queen Anne's Bounty to be applied for the benefit of the incumbent, if the owner be the incumbent of a benefice. Provision is made for the redemption of the rent

The Commutation Act of 1836.

charge in other cases of ownership. If a tenant had contracted, before the passing of the Act, to pay the extraordinary rent charge to the owner, he shall do so no longer, but pay to his landlord during his tenancy the rent charge substituted for the extraordinary charge. The landlord is then made liable for the payment of the rent charge to the owner, notwithstanding any agreement to the contrary which the tenant had made with his landlord. The Ecclesiastical Commissioners are empowered to adjust the fixed charges made, before the passing of this Act, on the income of benefices in receipt of extraordinary tithes in favour of other benefices, or of district churches or chapelries within the parishes of which the incumbents are in receipt of extraordinary tithes.

Lord John Russell, in introducing the Tithe Commutation Bill, said these words : " The income of the clergy will now flow from the landlord and not from the farmer, and the clergyman will be relieved from an alternative that too often exists, either of making personal enemies by pressing his demand, or of injuring himself by abandoning it."

His lordship, in his " Recollections and Suggestions," makes the following statement :—" All the evils of the tithe system were the subject of fair compromise and permanent settlement by the

Act of 1836. Three commissioners, two of whom were appointed by the Crown and one by the Archbishop of Canterbury, were empowered, after examination, to proceed by certain fixed rules to a final adjudication. In about seven years this process was completed, and a work from which Pitt had shrunk was accomplished."

In reading this statement one may smile at the "permanent settlement." Ever since 1836 there has been a continuous struggle going on down to 1886 on the subject of "extraordinary tithe rent charge." And even the dual landlordism which the Act created, will lead to further amendments of the Act. It will be necessary to make other alterations in the Act, so it is far from being a "permanent settlement."

The SEPTENNIAL AVERAGE PRICES of WHEAT, BARLEY, and OATS from 1835 to 1885, or 50 years, taken from Willich's Tithe Commutation Tables.

Per London Gazette	WHEAT, per imperial bushel.		BARLEY, per imperial bushel.		OATS, per imperial bushel.		Value of TITHE RENT CHARGE of £100.		
	s.	d.	s.	d.	s.	d.	£	s.	d.
To Christmas 1835 on 9th Dec. 1836	7	0¼	3	11½	2	9	100	0	0
To Christmas 1836 on 13th Jan. 1837	6	8½	3	11¾	2	9	98	13	9¾
To Christmas 1837 on 12th Jan. 1838	6	6¾	3	11¼	2	8¾	97	7	11
To Christmas 1838 on 4th Jan. 1839	6	6¼	3	9¾	2	8	95	7	9
To Christmas 1839 on 3rd Jan. 1840	6	9	3	11¼	2	9½	98	15	9½
To Christmas 1840 on 8th Jan. 1841	6	11¾	4	1	2	10¾	102	12	5¼
To Christmas 1841 on 7th Jan. 1842	7	3¾	4	2	2	11¼	105	8	2¾
To Christmas 1842 on 6th Jan. 1843	7	7½	4	1¼	2	10½	10,	12	2¼
To Christmas 1843 on 5th Jan. 1844	7	7¾	4	0½	2	9½	104	3	5¼
To Christmas 1844 on 3rd Jan. 1845	7	7	4	1¼	2	9	103	17	11½
To Christmas 1845 on 2nd Jan. 1846	7	4	4	1¾	2	9	102	17	8¾
To Christmas 1846 on 1st Jan. 1847	7	0¼	4	0	2	8¼	99	18	10¼
To Christmas 1847 on 7th Jan. 1848	7	1¼	4	1½	2	9½	102	1	0
To Christmas 1848 on 5th Jan. 1849	6	11¼	4	1¼	2	8¾	100	3	7¾
To Christmas 1849 on 8th Jan. 1850	6	7¼	4	1¼	2	8¼	98	16	10
To Christmas 1850 on 3rd Jan. 1851	6	5¼	4	0	2	8	96	11	4½
To Christmas 1851 on 2nd Jan. 1852	6	2¾	3	10¼	2	7¼	93	16	11¼
To Christmas 1852 on 7th Jan. 1853	6	0¼	3	9¼	2	6¾	91	13	5¾
To Christmas 1853 on 6th Jan. 1854	6	0	3	9¼	2	6¾	90	19	5
To Christmas 1854 on 5th Jan. 1855	6	0¾	3	7¾	2	6	8	15	8¾
To Christmas 1855 on 11th Jan 1856	6	6	3	8½	2	7¼	93	18	1¼
To Christmas 1856 on 9th Jan. 1857	6	11¼	3	11¼	2	9¼	99	13	7¼
To Christmas 1857 on 8th Jan 1858	7	2¼	4	3½	2	11	105	16	3¼
To Christmas 1858 on 7th Jan. 1859	7	4	4	5¼	3	0¼	108	19	6¼
To Christmas 1859 on 6th Jan. 1860	7	4½	4	6¼	3	1¼	110	17	8¼
To Christmas 1860 on 1th Jan. 1861	7	4¼	4	7¼	3	2	112	3	4¾
To Christmas 1861 on 10th Jan. 1862	7	0¾	4	7¼	3	1	1'9	13	6
To Christmas 1862 on 9th Jan. 1863	6	8¾	4	7½	3	0	107	5	2
To Christmas 1863 on 8th Jan. 1864	6	3½	4	1½	2	1¼	103	3	10¾
To Christmas 1864 on 30th Dec. 1864	6	0	4	3¼	2	10	98	15	10¼
To Christmas 1865 on 9th Jan. 1866	5	11¼	4	2¼	2	9½	97	7	9¼
To Christmas 1866 on 8th Jan. 1867	6	0¾	4	3	2	9¾	98	13	8
To Christmas 1867 on 7th Jan. 1868	6	3¼	4	3¾	2	10¼	100	13	9
To Christmas 1868 on 5th Jan. 1869	6	5¼	4	5¼	2	11	103	5	8¼
To Christmas 1869 on 4th Jan. 1870	6	3½	4	6¼	2	11¾	104	1	0¼
To Christmas 1870 on 10th Jan. 1871	6	4	4	6¼	3	0¼	104	15	1
To Christmas 1871 on 9th Jan. 1872	6	7½	4	7¼	3	1¼	108	4	0¼
To Christmas 1872 on 7th Jan. 1873	6	10¾	4	9	3	1¼	110	15	10¼
To Christmas 1873 on 6th Jan. 1874	7	0¼	4	10	3	1¾	112	7	3
To Christmas 1874 on 5th Jan. 1875	6	10¾	4	11	3	2¼	111	15	6¾
To Christmas 1875 on 4th Jan. 1876	6	6¾	4	10	3	2¼	110	14	11
To Christmas 1876 on 2nd Jan. 1877	6	6¼	4	9	3	2¼	10)	16	11¾
To Christmas 1877 on 1st Jan. 1878	6	8½	4	10¼	3	3¼	112	7	5¼
To Christmas 1878 on 7th Jan. 1879	6	6¼	4	11	3	3	111	15	1¼
To Christmas 1879 on 6th Jan. 1880	6	3½	4	10¼	3	2¼	10)	17	9¼
To Christmas 1880 on 4th Jan. 1881	6	0¼	4	8¼	3	2¼	107	2	10¼
To Christmas 1881 on 3rd Jan. 1882	5	10¾	4	6	3	0¾	102	16	2
To Christmas 1882 on 2nd Jan. 1883	5	10¾	4	4¼	2	11¼	100	4	9¾
To Christmas 1883 on 1st Jan. 1884	5	9¼	4	3	2	10¼	98	6	2¼
To Christmas 1884 on 6th Jan. 1885	5	4¾	4	1¾	2	9	93	17	3
To Christmas 1885 on 5th Jan. 1886	5	1¾	3	11¾	2	8¼	90	10	3½
							50) £129	10	6½
General Average for the last 50 years							£102	11	9½

Tithe Rent Charge in Wales.

Of the gross revenue of £14,000 a year which the bishops of St Asaph and Bangor received in 1836, over £11,000 came from the tithes of the parishes which were within their respective dioceses. The Bishop of Bangor stated in the House of Lords, that these tithes which the two bishops possessed, had never belonged to the clergy. He must have meant that they were never granted to parishes, but appropriated to the two bishoprics by the original benefactors.

In 1831 there were four parishes in North Wales, covering 47 square miles, with a population of 4631, which were annexed with their tithes to an English monastery before the Reformation. At the Dissolution those churches and their tithes were transferred to the bishopric of Lichfield and Coventry. It was a common practice for King Henry VIII. and his successors to exchange tithes for estates, and then to transfer the estates to their ministers and courtiers, or to sell them, as Elizabeth did, to furnish money for the public service, instead of applying to Parliament. The four vicars of the four appropriated Welsh parishes received in 1831 the grand sum of £429 per annum!! a little over £100 a year for each.

The tithes of Welshpool and of other parishes in Montgomeryshire were annexed at the Reformation to the Dean and Chapter of Christ Church, Oxford. The see of Chester received two-thirds of the tithes of Carnarvon and the vicar one-third. Jesus College, Oxford, received tithes of some of the parishes in Bangor. These are but a few specimens of how the tithes in Wales, and especially in North Wales, are appropriated to bishops, colleges, and cathedral chapters, and they explain the cause of the wretched salaries which are paid to many of the Welsh vicars.

Fifty years ago the Church in Wales was in a most wretched condition. The sees, cathedral dignities, and best livings were filled by Englishmen, some of whom may have been good "Grecians" or "Romans," but were terribly bad Welshmen. They did not know a word of the language of the people. They were aliens in blood, in manners, and language from the great bulk of the population. It is a fact that the rites of confirmation, baptisms, marriages, prayers and preaching, were performed through interpreters!! Now, it is distinctly laid down in the twenty-fourth article of the Church of England, that "it is a thing plainly repugnant to the Word of God and the custom of the primitive Church to have public prayers in the church or to minister the sacraments in a tongue not understanded of the people." It is not to be wondered at that two-thirds of the people of Wales are Dissenters, and that the remaining one-third belong to the Established Church and are like the Protestant Episcopalians in Ireland before the Disestablishment. They were of the Church of the minority; so they are in Wales.

When the Church Reform Bill was passing through the House of Commons in 1836, a member moved, "That it be an instruction to the committee on the second reading that no clergyman not fully conversant with the Welsh language be appointed to any see or benefice in the principality of Wales." If that motion had been adopted fifty years ago and faithfully carried out, the Church in Wales would be in a much better position in the affections of the people than it is at the present time. Lord Chancellor Cottenham, who, before his elevation to the woolsack, had been a member of the Ecclesiastical Commission of Inquiry in 1835, and signed the reports, was terribly annoyed at the the above motion. "He considered it presumptuous for any person to interfere with his patronage in Wales." As a commissioner he must have been familiar with the terribly neglected condition of the Church in the principality in 1836. The fact

Retrospective View of Tithes in England. 137

is, that Crown patronage, *i.e.*, the patronage of the Prime Minister, appointing archbishops, bishops, deans, and a certain number of canons, coupled with the large patronage of benefices by the Crown and Lord, Chancellor, have been a terrible drag at all times on the progress of the Church of England.

Retrospective View of Tithes in England.

I shall now take a retrospective view of tithes in England—

(1.) In 855, when Ethelwulph's law was passed, the population of England and Wales could not be more than 750,000, and one million of acres under cultivation.

(2.) In 1066, population about one and a quarter millions, lands cultivated about one and a half million of acres.

(3.) In 1215, population about two millions, lands cultivated about two and half millions of acres.

(4.) In 1547, when Henry VIII. died, the population was about five millions, and about six millions of acres under cultivation.

(5.) The 2 and 3 Edw. VI., c. 13, s. 5, enacted that "all barren or waste ground which before this time have lain barren and paid no tithes by reason of the same barrenness, and now be, or hereafter shall be improved or converted into arable or meadow, shall, after the end of seven years next after such improvement, pay tithe for the corn and hay growing upon the same."

The common law would levy tithes immediately, and thus inflict an injustice upon the people who vested their capital to improve the land. When the Act was passed, only the one-fifth of the land was cultivated, or about six millions of acres. There are at present (1886) over twenty-six millions of acres under cultivation. Therefore, from 1548 to 1886, tithes, or tithe rent charges, have been paid on over twenty millions of acres of waste lands which were brought into cultivation. We are told that tithes were not created by Acts of Parliament, that they were paid before the English Parliament existed. But on how many acres were they paid before the existence of the English Parliament? Upon how many acres have they been paid by Edward's Act? Twenty millions. Were payment of tithes on these twenty millions of acres voluntary endowments made by the tenants or landlords? Let the "Brief" answer: "When waste land has been brought into cultivation, and the owners have sought to evade the payment of tithes, the State, by enactment or otherwise, has enforced the payment of that due to the Church" (p. 47). Now, Edward's Act stopped payment for seven years, which common law would demand at once. If it could stop payment for seven years, could it not stop payment for seventy times seven years, or for ever? Yes. Personal tithes are not now paid. The common-law right for their payment is as strong as that for the payment of predial tithes. By the Commutation Act of 1836 the landlords gained fully two millions of tithes, and the landlords of hop gardens gained £250,000 a year from tithes by the Act of 1862. It is certainly landlords' gain to pocket so many millions a year of tithes under the guise of improving or correcting or solving the tithe question whenever agitations on the subject arise. This fact is explained by another fact, that only Parliament can solve the question, and Parliament, being almost composed of landlords, solve tithe problems, of course, in their own interests, certainly not in the interests of the farmers or labourers.

CHAPTER XI.

TITHES IN THE CITY AND LIBERTIES OF LONDON.

IN the early history of the Christian Church, the citizens of London made oblations or offerings at every mass on Sundays and holidays, and such oblations were applied to the relief of the poor, the repairs of the church, and the support of the clergy. From these purely voluntary oblations grew up a custom in the City of London, that every person paying 20s. a year rental should give to God and the Church, ½d. for every Sunday or Apostles' Day, the vigil of which was a fast. If he paid only 10s. a year rental, he was to give ¼d. This amounted in the former case to 2s. 6d. in the pound, and 1s. 3d. in the latter per annum. These were customary payments, and were applied for the same usual three purposes, the poor, the Church, and the clergy. As these customary payments were found to decrease, it was deemed necessary to promulgate an order to permanently

Tithes in City and Liberties of London. 141

fix the customary payments. Bishop Roger took up the subject at once, immediately after his consecration as Bishop of London. The following are the facts of the case :—

(I.) In 1228, in the reign of Henry III., Bishop Roger, surnamed Niger, or Le Noir, of London, made a constitution, or modus, that every occupier of a house should offer as his tithe to his parish church ½d. for 20s. a year rental, and ¼d. for 10s. a year rental, for every Sunday and every apostle's day whereof the evening was fasted. There were fifty-two Sundays and eight apostles' days in the year that were fasted. Two shillings and sixpence a year was then the amount of the modus decimandi which the former occupier had to pay, and 1s. 3d. a year the latter. The amounts would be less when any of the apostles' days fell upon Sundays.

The above particulars appear in the Records of London. It is a well-known point in law that a house *quâ* house is not liable for the payment of tithes. Tithes were paid for what issued or grew out of the ground. Enormous house properties have been built in and around all our cities and towns for which one penny as tithe money has not been paid, and yet the house property in the city and liberty of London and landed property throughout the country have to pay tithes. Add to this the fact that about one-fourth of the whole tithe rent charge, or nearly one million of money, goes to lay impropriators, colleges, schools, &c.; and again, add another fact, that large landed properties are exempted by Henry VIII.'s Act from paying any tithes at all.

Bishop Roger's modus was paid for 160 years, viz., from 1229 to 1389, when Archbishop Arundell of Canterbury interfered with the arrangement in the latter year. He was not satisfied with the interpretation put upon Bishop Roger's constitution as regards the number of apostles' days, and so he added twenty-two more saints' days, thus increasing the tithe payments from 2s. 6d. to 3s. 5d. a year, and this he did without consulting the payers. The citizens of London were quite indignant at the additional number of saints' days, and placed on record their protest against the same for the information of future generations. There were constant quarrels between the citizens and their clergy in the ecclesiastical courts and at the pope's court at Rome as to the payment of the extra 11d. The archbishop appealed to the pope as to the soundness of his interpretation, and, as a matter of course, Pope Innocent VII. in 1403 confirmed the interpretation. But the pope's bull did not pacify the citizens of London. They considered the additional 11d. as a cheat—a fraud. Besides, the pope's

Tithes in City and Liberties of London. 143

bull could not compel them to pay the additional amount. However, in 1453, it appears, by a record in the Town-Clerk's Office (Letter Book K., 32 Henry VI.) that Archbishop Arundell's order is declared by the Common Council to be "destructory rather than declaratory, and that it was obtained surreptitiously and deceptiously, without assent on the part of the citizens, or summoning them." I should imagine the Church, with its terrible ecclesiastical courts, made them pay the 3s. 5d., for we find no change in the payment until we come to (II.) 1535, when the whole subject was considered by the Privy Council, who made an order for the payment of 2s. 9d. in the pound. Therefore in the same year an Act of Parliament (27 Henry VIII., c. 21) was passed, authorising the citizens of London to pay their tithes at the rate of 2s. 9d. in the pound. Ten years later another Act was passed (37 Henry VIII., c. 12), " That the citizens and inhabitants of the city of London and liberties of the same shall yearly, without fraud or covin, for ever pay their tithes to the parsons, vicars, and curates of the said city, and their successors for the time being, after the following rate:—For every 10s. rent by the year of all houses, shops, warehouses, cellars, stables, &c., within the city and liberty, 16½d.; and for every 20s. rent by the year, 2s. 9d.; and so above the rent of 20s. by the year, ascending from 10s. to 10s., according to the rate aforesaid."

The parson's or appropriator's share of the tithes in London before the Reformation was 9d. in the pound. Strictly speaking, tithes on houses for habitation had not been paid by "Common Law." As I stated in the first page, tithes were only due of things that grew, increased, and renewed from year to year. Houses did not increase in value as a general rule, but rather decreased.

When leases are made, it is enacted that tenants or farmers shall pay their tithes after the above rate, according to the rents they paid when last let before making such leases.

The tithes were to be paid quarterly, viz., at Easter, Nativity of St John Baptist, Michaelmas, and Christmas.

The householder who paid his tithes was discharged of paying any of the four offering days, but his wife, children, servant, and others of their family taking the rights of the Church at Easter were to pay 2d. for their four offering days yearly. In all Acts of Parliament dealing generally with tithes, from the reign of Henry VIII. to the present time, the city and liberty of London were always excluded from the Acts, for their tithes were dealt with separately.

Tithes in City and Liberties of London. 145

(III.) The next account of tithes in London was after the great fire of 1666.

An Act was passed (22 and 23 Charles II., c. 15) for the better settlement of the maintenance of the parsons, vicars, and curates in the parishes of the city of London burnt by the great fire:

"Whereas the tithes in the city of London were levied and paid with great inequality, and are, since the late dreadful fire there, in the rebuilding of the same, by taking away some houses, altering the foundations of many, and the new erecting of others, so disordered, that in case they should not for the time to come be reduced to a certainty, many contrivances and suits of law might arise, be it enacted that the annual certain tithes of every parish in the city of London and its liberties, whose churches have been demolished or in part consumed by the late fire, be paid according to the sum opposite each." Then the names of fifty-one parishes follow with sums ranging from £100 to £200 per annum, each in lieu of tithes.

Sec. 3. "Which respective sums of money to be paid in lieu of tithes within the said respective parishes, and assessed as hereinafter is directed, shall be and continue to be esteemed, deemed, and taken to all intents and purposes, to be the

K

respective annual maintenance (over and above glebes and perquisites, gifts and bequests to the respective parson, vicar, and curate of any parish for the time being, or to their successors respectively, or to others for their use), of the said respective parsons, vicars, and curates who shall be legally instituted, inducted, and admitted in the respective parishes aforesaid."

In subsequent sections, assessments were ordered to be made before 24th July 1671, upon all houses, shops, warehouses, cellars, and other hereditaments, except parsonage and vicarage houses.

Three transcripts were to be made by the assessors, containing the respective sums to be payable out of all the premises within each parish; one was for the lord mayor, the second for the bishop of London's registry, and the third was to remain in the vestry. The payments were to be made in four quarterly payments.

If any inhabitant should refuse payment, the lord mayor should issue his warrant of distress on his goods. If the lord mayor should refuse to issue his warrant, then it shall be lawful for the Lord Chancellor or Keeper of the Great Seal, or any two or more of the barons of his Majesty's Court of Exchequer, to issue warrants of distress.

St Bartholomew's Hospital, London, was founded

Tithes in City and Liberties of London. 147

by Henry VIII., who gave the hospital the impropriate rectory and tithes of the parish of Christ Church, Newgate Street, in the city of London.

The inhabitants of those parishes within the city of London and its liberties, which were not destroyed by the fire of 1666, were compelled by the parsons and impropriators of such parishes, to pay 2s. 9d. in the pound upon the rentals of their houses. These individuals were never entitled to all this sum for their own immediate use and benefit, but the whole sum was paid into the common treasury of the parish, and was applied to three distinct and separate purposes, viz. : (1) The relief of the poor ; (2) the repairs of the church ; and (3) the support of the clergy. [Report of the Special Committee in relation to Tithes, submitted to the Court of Common Council, May 1812, City Records.] .

(IV.) By the Christ Church (City) Tithe Act, 1879 (42 and 43 Vic., c. 93), the hospital was to receive in lieu of tithes the annual sum of £1800, which shall be levied and collected as tithe rates by the hospital, or and from the persons by law rateable to poor rates in that parish.

Christ Hospital, which is within the parish, shall pay £100 a year to the governors of St Bartholomew's. Tithes in arrears are recoverable by distress in the same manner as stated in the Commutation Act of 1836.

The charter constituting the hospital provided that the governors should pay five priests in celebrating divine service in the parish church each £8 a-year, and the Act of 1879 stated above, allowed them, if they thought fit, to pay the vicar of Christ Church £150 a year out of the £1800, in addition to the £40 already paid.

(V.) The City of London Tithes Act of 1879 (42 and 43 Vic., c. 176) provides for the commutation of tithes and payments in lieu of tithes arising or growing due in certain parishes in the city of London, and for the redemption of rent charges charged upon lands under the above Act.

(VI.) Mr Edward Jeffries Esdaile and his successors are the owners of the tithes of the parish of St-Botolph-Without, Aldgate. Disputes arose after the Act of 1879 as to the payments to be made to Mr Esdaile in respect of tithes; an Act was therefore passed in 1881, entitled, "The City of London Tithes, St-Botolph-Without, Aldgate" (44 and 45 Vic., c. 197), to commute the tithes.

By sec. 3 of this Act, the tithe-owner is to receive £6500 a year in lieu of tithes, and which was to be levied and collected by the churchwardens from the persons by law rateable to poor

Tithes in City and Liberties of London. 149

rates, and shall be assessed on the annual rateable value of the house assessed for poor rates. The £6500 a-year was to be paid by the churchwardens to the tithe-owner after 29th September 1881 by two half-yearly payments, the first to be made on 25th March 1882.

The cost of making and collecting the tithe-rates is to be paid by the ratepayers, and is to be exclusive of the £6500.

The owners of houses can redeem the tithes as if they were rent charge under the Tithes Commutation Act of 1836.

A meeting was held in 1880, before the Act was passed, at which it was agreed by the ratepayers to commute the tithes for the sum of £4000, which was afterwards increased to £5000; but when the Bill was passing through Parliament the sum was changed to £6500, because the promoters of the Bill said that the tithe-owner was entitled to 2s. 9d. in the pound on £89,000, the amount of valuation, whereas the actual value of the parish was £56,957, and in 1886 the value was lower. Mr Esdaile purchased the tithes for £20,000, for which he receives £6500 a-year, or $32\frac{1}{2}$ per cent. on the purchase money. The result of the Act of 1881 is to increase the tithe-rates on each occupier, as people feel reluctant to rent or purchase property in a parish so heavily taxed for tithe rates. This will of course account for the diminution instead of the anticipated increase in the value of the rateable property in this parish, and will also account for the tithe-rates being in 1886 nearly the double of what they were before the Act was passed.

CHAPTER XII.

REDEMPTION OF TITHE RENT CHARGE.

THE following statement is taken from the Tithe Commissioners' Report for the year 1882:—

Payable to Clerical Appropriators,	£678,987	1	1¾
„ Parochial Incumbents,	2,412,708	9	11¼
„ Lay Impropriators, .	766,233	0	6¾
„ Schools and Colleges,	196,056	15	0½
Total, . .	£4,053,985	6	8⅓

Owing to agricultural depression its value in 1886 was but £3,668,857 gross. If 20 per cent. be allowed for collection, rates, and taxes, the net value was £2,935,086. It is proposed to redeem this at twenty years' purchase, or £58,701,720, which, if invested in consols at 3 per cent., will produce an income of £1,761,051. It is further proposed that the landlords should borrow from the Government the redemption money at 4 per cent., so that in forty years they should have repaid the Government both principal and interest. By this mode the land in England and

Wales would for ever be free from the payment of tithes.

The Clerical Appropriators are—

The Archbishops and Bishops whose gross tithes are, in round numbers,	£190,000
The Chapters, do. do.,	310,000
The separate estates of Deans and Prebends vested in the Ecclesiastical Commissioners,	180,000
Total,	£680,000

All this is paid to the Ecclesiastical Commissioners.

The following statement gives the net revenues in 1886, under the following four headings, after deducting $9\frac{1}{2}$ per cent. depreciation in value, 5 per cent. for collection, and $15\frac{1}{2}$ per cent. for rates, taxes, &c. :—

Clerical Appropriators,	£488,872 net.
Parochial Incumbents,	1,737,151
Lay Impropriators,	551,688
Schools, Colleges, &c.,	141,161
Total,	£2,918,872

As Lay Impropriators, Schools, Colleges, &c., are not engaged in the spiritual work of the Established Church, we must add only the first two to

Redemption of Tithe Rent Charge. 153

obtain the net sum which the clerical staff of the Church receive from tithe rent charge, viz.. £488,872 + £1,737,151 = £2,226,023. To this sum must be added (£8000—£1600 for expenses) £6400 for extraordinary tithe rent charge, and we get £2,232,423. It is not fair to credit the bishops, chapters, and parochial incumbents with the tithes received by laymen, schools, colleges, hospitals, &c. The capital value at twenty-five years' purchase for the actual Church revenue is £2,232,423 × 25 = £55,810,575, or fifty-six millions in round numbers, which, if invested in consols at 3 per cent., will give an income of £1,674,317, or say £1,675,000 per annum. These are stubborn facts, mathematically correct.

The following statement gives the capital sums and yearly incomes under the four headings as arranged above, on the redemption scale of twenty years' purchase:—

	Capital sum at 20 years purchase.	Yearly income at 3 per cent.
Clerical Appropriators,	£9,777,440	£293,323
Parochial Incumbents,	34,871,020	1,046,130
Lay Impropriators,	11,033,760	331,013
Schools, Colleges, &c.,	2,823,220	84,697
Total,	£58,505,440	£1,755,163

At twenty-five years' purchase the value of the

redemption would be £73,131,800, which at 3 per cent. Consols would produce an income of £2,193,954.

	Capital sum at 25 years' purchase.	Yearly income at 3 per cent. Consols.
Clerical Appropriators,	£12,221,800	£366,654
Parochial Incumbents,	43,588,775	1,307,663
Lay Impropriators,	13,792,200	413,766
Schools, Colleges, &c.,	3,529,025	105,871
Total,	£73,131,800	£2,193,954

Twenty years' purchase annually for church staff will produce £1,339,453, twenty-five years' purchase annually for church staff will produce £1,674,317 ; or in round numbers respectively £1,340,000 and £1,675,000. Amount received in 1886 was £2,226,023. By the twenty years' purchase, the church staff would lose in income (£2,226,023 − £1,339,453)=£886,570, and by twenty-five years' purchase (£2,226,023−£1,674,317)=£551,706. I omit all calculations for the other tithe owners, because I am strongly of opinion that their rent charges should go to satisfy local claims such as the education of the farmers' children.

I mean by Church staff the archbishops, bishops, deans, canons, and parochial incumbents.

TITHE RENT CHARGE FOR 1887, &c.

There appeared in the *London Gazette* of January 4, 1887, the following return, stating what has been, during the seven years ending Christmas Day 1886, the price of an imperial bushel of British wheat, barley, and oats, viz.—

	s.	d.
Wheat,	4	11
Barley,	3	10
Oats,	2	7½

From these data, I have calculated the tithe rent charge to be £87, 8s. 9¾d. for the year 1887. It is more than 12½ per cent. below par value, and 3 per cent. less than the previous year. The following table indicates the gross and net values of the tithe rent charge for 1887:—

	Gross value of tithe rent charge for 1887, including £8000 extraordinary rent charge.	Net value, after allowing 5 per cent. for collection, and 1¼ per cent. for rates, taxes, and other expenses attached to tithe rent.
	£	£
Clerical Appropriators,	593,699	471,991
Parochial Incumbents, .	2,117,611	1,683,500
Lay Impropriators, . . .	669,975	532,631
Schools, Colleges, &c.,	171,426	136,284
Total, ...	3,552,711	2,824,406

The following table will give the capital sums and incomes at 3 per cent. on 20 and 25 years' purchase respectively upon the above net values. It would be absurd, as I said before, to calculate the purchase money on the par value of the tithe rent charge.

	Capital sum at 20 years' purchase.	Income of Capital on 20 years' purchase at 3 per cent.	Capital sum at 25 years' purchase.	Income of Capital on 25 years' purchase at 3 per cent.
	£	£	£	£
Clerical Appropriators,	9,439,820	283,194	11,799,775	353,994
Parochial Incumbents,	33,670,000	1,010,100	42,087,500	1,262,625
Lay Impropriators, .	10,652,920	319,587	13,316,150	399,483
Schools, Colleges, &c.,	2,725,780	81,773	3,407,225	102,216
Total, . .	56,488,520	1,694,654	70,610,650	2,118,318

In 1887 the Church staff receive from tithe rent charges, net, . . . £2,155,491

The income of staff, if rent charge be redeemed at 20 years' purchase at 3 per cent., ... = 1,293,294

The income of staff, if rent charge be redeemed at 25 years' purchase at 3 per cent., ... = 1,616,619

By 20 years' purchase, the staff will lose in income £862,197 per annum, calculated on the value of the tithe rent charge for 1887. By 25 years' purchase the loss would be only £538,872, but a permanent income would be obtained, free from

Redemption of Tithe Rent Charge.

all future disputes between the clergy and their parishioners, or from extraneous sources.

According to the Tithe Commissioners' Report for 1882, the value of the tithe rent charge at par value, for Church staff was, including £8000 extraordinary tithe, . . . = £3,099,695
Gross value in 1887, . . = 2,711,310

Gross loss in 1887, . = £388,385
Of this loss, £303,097 fall on the parochial clergy, and £85,288 on the Ecclesiastical Commissioners, who are now owners of the tithe rent charge (of 1887) of £593,699, belonging to bishops and chapters.

REDEMPTION VIEWED FROM ANOTHER POINT.

There is another point from which the redemption may be viewed. The landlord is legally bound to pay the rent charge, and Parliament may pass a short Act making void all engagements with tenants on the part of landlords to pay the rent charge, and also repeal the clause in the Commutation Act as regards distraints on the lands for arrears of rent charge. The security for rent charge is safe and solid. The rent charge for 1887 is 12½ per cent. below par value. It may go lower for a few years, but it is sure to take an upward turn, and approximate to par, or even go beyond it, as it did before. The net income of the Church staff for 1887 is £2,155,491. It may reasonably be asked, Why should the purchase money be calculated upon the depreciation of value of the rent charge, plus the expenses? The rent charge is sure to take an upward turn, then, Why should not the purchase money be calculated on the rent charge at par value *minus* the expenses for collection, rates, taxes, repairs of chancels, &c., say 20½ per cent.?

From this reasonable point of view, the following table will indicate capital sums and incomes on 20 and 25 years' purchase respectively, on amounts after deducting 20½ per cent. from the par value.

	Amount after deducting 20½ per cent. from par value for expenses.
Clerical Appropriators,	£ 539,795
Parochial Incumbents,	1,924,463
Lay Impropriators,	609,156
Schools, Colleges, &c.,	155,865
Total,	3,229,279

Redemption of Tithe Rent Charge. 159

	Capital on 20 years' purchase.	Income at 3 per cent on Capital of 20 years' purchase.	Capital on 25 years' purchase.	Income at 3 per cent. on Capital of 25 years' purchase.
	£	£	£	£
Clerical Appropriators,	10,795,900	323,877	13,494,875	404,846
Parochial Incumbents,	38,489,260	1,154,678	48,111,575	1,443,348
Lay Impropriators, .	12,183,120	365,493	15,228,900	456,867
Schools, Colleges, &c.,	3,117,300	93,519	3,896,625	116,898
Total, . . .	64,585,580	1,937,567	80,731,975	2,421,959

By this arrangement, Church staff's income, 20 years' purchase, . . . = £1,478,555
Do. 25 do., = 1,848,194
Their net income at par value, . = 2,464,258
Their net income in 1887, . = 2,155,491

LAY IMPROPRIATORS, SCHOOLS, COLLEGES, ETC.

The income of Lay Impropriators, Schools, Colleges—

Net income at par value of rent charge, . £765,021
Net income for 1887, ... 668,915
    Do. on 20 years' purchase of the rent charge for 1887, . . . 401,360
    Do. on 25 years' purchase of the rent charge for 1887, . . . 501,699
    Do. on 20 years' purchase on rent charge at par value, . . 459,012
    Do. on 25 years' purchase on rent charge at par value, . . 573,765

The best way to dispose of this annual revenue is to expend it on the education of the children of parents of all denominations who reside on the lands which pay the tithe rent charges. That could easily be arranged in a few clauses of the Redemption Act. It should not be devoted to decreasing the rates and taxes, or given to school-boards, and thus decrease school rates, for some landlords would take advantage of such reductions, and raise their rents accordingly. But it should be exclusively spent in freeing the parents from weekly cash fees, building better schools, providing better school furniture, reducing price of books, and employing better teachers. Half a million a year thus expended from such sources, would, I am certain, be more productive of benefit to the country than it is at present. The essence of the Christian religion is to provide for the poor and not for the rich, who can very well and did take care of themselves "in going in" for large slices of church spoliation.

The redemption scheme is no doubt the best mode of solving this difficult problem. But an important question will arise—Why should our well endowed universities and public schools receive the large sums set opposite their names from localities where it would be of great use if employed in

Redemption of Tithe Rent Charge. 161

satisfying local claims in educating the children of those places? Those who send their sons to the public schools and universities, are well able to pay for their education. Why, then, should not the money be devoted to the education of the farmers' children of the localities from which the tithes arise? These remarks are equally strong, if not more so, against lay impropriators. They give no return whatever for the large annual revenues they take from the lands. Are not the rentals of the confiscated monastic lands without the tithes ample enough? Parliament sanctioned the confiscation. But there is a mighty difference between the Parliaments of Henry VIII. and of Queen Victoria. The tithes of the lay impropriators should also go to satisfy the educational local claims where they arise. The remarks are not so strong against the clerical appropriators and parochial incumbents. The high-handed conduct of Henry VIII., Edward VI., and Elizabeth, deprived many of the bishops of large portions of their landed estates, and gave them monastic tithes in return, instead of giving them back to the parochial clergy. This accounts for the large episcopal revenues derived from tithes. The rich estates thus taken from the bishops were partly handed over by these sovereigns to their favourites and courtiers, and partly sold by Queen Elizabeth to replenish the national exchequer, as she was averse to the practice of resorting to Parliament for money for national purposes. The nation thus derived a pecuniary benefit from part of the episcopal estates. It is therefore only just that the bishops should enjoy the revenues derived from the redemption money. The bishops had a far better title to their landed estates than the Duke of Bedford and many others to their monastic properties. Many of the bishops were compelled by law to exchange their landed property for parochial tithes. Therefore the bishops have a just claim on their tithes. It would have been very different if they received these tithes without such exchange of property under the compulsion of an Act of Parliament. If people say they should be deprived of the revenues of such tithes, then the Duke of Bedford and others possessing monastic lands and tithes should also be compelled to surrender them to the nation. In reference to the parochial incumbents, the Ecclesiastical Commissioners, as the Church corporation, would be the distributors of the revenue of over one million a year. This should be carefully restricted to satisfying local claims, for the original donors never intended that the tithes of their estates or any part of them should be devoted to the maintenance of incumbents unconnected with the churches upon their estates. There is a vast sphere of work for the commissioners in diminishing the large incomes of the rectors of mother churches, and adequately increasing those of the incumbents of the daughter churches. Besides such funds will enable them to stimulate the spiritual work in such localities by building new churches and mission rooms, and adequately remunerating those employed in the work. I do not think the Nonconformist bodies would seriously object to this arrangement as regards the parochial clergy. From a million to a million and a quarter a year is not much among so many rural incumbents. The redemption scheme would finally settle a much vexed question.

All the changes made by Parliament since 1836 in the payment of tithes or tithe rent charges have always been to the profit of the landlords. The Commutation Act of 1836 gave them two millions of profits; to this sum we may add a half million more by subsequent changes. The redemption scheme would for ever put an end to further profits by the landlords. But the proposed twenty years purchase should be increased to twenty-five years.

The security for the payment of the tithe-rent

charge by the Act of 1836 is so substantial that the redemption price should not be less than twenty-five years' purchase. We must also consider that the landlords have profited by the changes made in the payment of tithes in 1836 and subsequent years by a sum not less than two and a half millions a year. From 1836 to about 1882 they made no abatements of any consequence, but enjoyed their full profits from tithes of from two to two and a half millions a year plus fifteen millions of increased rentals. But abatements in rents are not permanent reductions in rents. Besides, the Tithe Commutation Act gave a remarkable impetus to agricultural improvements, which tended vastly to increase the landlords' rentals to the amount stated above.

No doubt the large abatements which the landlords have given in their rentals on account of agricultural depression, take away almost all the profits which they derived from the changes in paying tithes and the high rentals. Yet they enjoyed all these profits and increasing rentals from 1836 up to about 1882.

CHAPTER XIII.

SOME REMARKS ON "A DEFENCE OF THE CHURCH OF ENGLAND AGAINST DISESTABLISHMENT," BY THE EARL OF SELBORNE. NEW EDITION. 1887.

WHEN the sheets of this work had just passed through the press, Lord Selborne's book was published. It contains many passages at variance with the views which I have expressed in this work. It was impossible for me, under the circumstances, to combat his lordship's statements at the proper places in the body of the text. I have, therefore, added a chapter specially dealing with those parts of his lordship's book which, as regards tithes and their division, are opposed to the views which I have expressed here.

(1.) His lordship says (p. 131), that "There is no historical foundation for the *idle story* told by some of the old chroniclers, and repeated by some *uncritical writers* in more modern times, about a supposed grant of all the tithes of his kingdom to the Church by King Offa, by way of penance for the murder which he had committed." How are we to draw the line in the old chroniclers between what is an "idle" story and what is a true one? Are the *critical* supporters of tithes and defenders of the Church at liberty to dub as "idle" stories the statements of our old chroniclers, when such statements militate against their prejudiced opinions? As one of the "uncritical" writers, I maintain that there is a much more solid historical foundation for the "idle story" about King Offa, than there is in that sinful perversion of Scripture about Adam having paid tithes, or that the Apostles received tithes, or that Archbishop Augustine and his missionaries received tithes according to that very "uncritical" defender of tithes, Archdeacon Tillesley; or that "The English bishops received tithes from the people as early as A.D. 747" (p. 129). The fact of the matter is, the story of Offa's gift of tithes to the Church to atone for the crime of murder which he committed, is viewed by Church defenders and supporters of tithes with such abhorrence, that they, as "critical" writers, repudiate the so-called "idle story" of our old chroniclers. They are utterly ashamed of any gift of tithes being given to the Church to atone for so foul a crime as murder. Lord Selborne therefore repudiates the unpalatable statement. We, "uncritical" writers, find, of course, no "idle stories" by old ecclesiastical writers and monks, setting forth the origin of tithes and the pretended miracles for their payment. I prefer to be "uncritical" than a believer in the false miracles recorded in Bede's "Ecclesiastical History," or those miracles recorded as having been performed by Archbishop Dunstan, or the stories about the payment of tithes concocted by monks in their cells, or forged canons and letters in support of tithes emanating from the same quarter. Yet "critical" Church defenders are not ashamed of parading before the public such productions in support of their opinion.

(2.) His lordship also ignores King Ethelwulph's charter. If this king made no law on the subject of tithes, why did so many of his successors confirm the law? We are told (p. 131) that Athelstan "grounded his order to pay tithes on certain texts of Scripture and of St Ambrose;" Ethelwulph's charter, which is ignored, has also a scriptural basis. His charters no doubt have been in a very mutilated state. Dean Prideaux, in his work, "Original and Right of Tithes," states that on Ethelwulph's charter "the civil right of tithes in this land had its main foundation." In this the dean is mistaken. In chapter iv., and other parts of this book, I have explained the origin of tithes in England—how they were first given as a customary free-will offering, and how this custom generated a common right.

(3.) Lord Selborne says (p. 149), "It is necessary for those who maintain that opinion [the division of tithes] to show by historical evidence that at some time or other in all or some part of England any such custom or practice did, in fact, prevail: and this has never been, and never can be done." I have given seven reasons in this book (pp. 27-29) for the division of tithes. I could have added an eighth from the custom adopted in London (chapter xi.). The Constitutions of Ethelred the Unready are undoubted "historical evidence," and are as genuine as any "historical evidence" which Lord Selborne in his book has produced in support of his own arguments or opinions. Lord Selborne takes up certain views, as regards the division of tithes, in defence of the Church. He ignores any claim on the tithes for the poor or the fabric of the Church. He maintains that the parson has the full right to all his tithes without any division whatsoever. These are the positions he takes up. As a special pleader and an *ex parte* writer, he pooh-poohs "historical

Defence of the Church of England. 169

evidence" as "idle stories" which militate against his own peculiar views. He dubs all as "uncritical writers" who will not read historical documents with his own spectacles. His lordship quotes passages from the works of certain authors in support of his own opinions, but when he finds passages in the *same* works which contradict any of his own peculiar theories, he disparages the statements. I shall give a few instances out of several to illustrate what I have thus asserted. He is profuse in his quotations from Johnson's "Laws and Canons" in support of his views, but when he comes to the collection of canons attributed to Archbishop Egbert, he says, "The tendency of Mr Johnson, and of other ecclesiastical writers of the seventeenth century (see Spelman, p. 132, and Stillingfleet, Eccles. Cases, etc., p. 89), was to accept ancient documents of this kind [meaning the collection of canons attributed to Archbishop Egbert] not on tithes only, but on other subjects also, with little discrimination" (Note, pp. 149, 150). From such observation one's confidence is much shaken in Mr Johnson's work when quoted by Lord Selborne himself in support of his own views. His animadversions are very strong. Mr Johnson uses very little discrimination, "not on tithes only, but on other subjects also." How then are we to believe that Mr Johnson is correct when his lordship quotes his work as an authority on his lordship's own side? I have stated my own opinion at p. 27, No. 3, on the collection of canons attributed to Archbishop Egbert. Again, Dean Prideaux is called an "uncritical writer" because he supports King Offa's grant of tithes and Ethelwulph's charter, both of which his lordship ignores; but the Dean is critical enough (pp. 136, 137) when his views harmonise with those of his lordship. His lordship's book is a most remarkable production of "special pleading" in defence of the Church. Selden, although a Puritan, has written, according to Lord Selborne, who is a great churchman, impartially on tithes. These are his lordship's words: "Of the English writers who have investigated this subject [of tithes] there has been none more learned, and *none more impartial*, than Selden. The best of our later common law authorities have followed him; I shall not scruple, generally, to do the same" (p. 137). Is Lord Selborne, like John Selden, impartial on the subject of tithes? I cannot say he is. There is a remarkable bias running in one direction through the whole book. He denies the tripartite or any other division of tithes, because there is no "historical evidence" to support such division in

Defence of the Church of England. 171

England. I have brought forward a Constitution of King Ethelred the Unready. It is genuine. How does Lord Selborne treat this "historical evidence"? Let himself answer. "Their ecclesiastical origin is evident: there is nothing to show that they [Ethelred's Constitutions, one of which treated on the tripartite division of tithes] were ever acted upon: and the portion of them material to the present question [the tripartite division] has no counterpart in any later (or earlier) Anglo-Saxon or Danish laws upon the same subject" (p. 152). Negative evidence never can upset positive "historical evidence." If one were disposed to argue from negative evidence, a great deal of his lordship's book, in my opinion, could be refuted.

This is not the way to convince the "critical" reader that the parson had the right to all the tithes, and that no part of them was set aside for the poor or the fabric of the Church.

Again, I have stated at p. 29, No. 7 (see also p. 54), Sir William Blackstone's remark on the Act of 1392 (15 Richard II. c. 6). That remark contains two statements: (1) Alms for the poor found one of the objects for which the payment of tithes was originally imposed; (2) the words "among other purposes," must imply more than the parson's share. It probably implied the repairs of the parish church.

In reference to this law, Lord Selborne says (p. 155) that it referred only to churches appropriated to monasteries, which were served by vicars. His lordship is of opinion that the fact of passing such a law proves that no law as regards the division of tithes then existed, otherwise such a law could be enforced without passing the Act 15 Richard II., c. 6. This is really expecting too much. Let us transport ourselves back to the fourteenth century, and examine the question as easily as we could in the nineteenth century, whether the machinery of the executive government of this country was then as perfect to enforce any existing law or custom for the protection and support of the poor as it is in the nineteenth century. I say most emphatically it was not. The parsons of the fourteenth century were well able to take care of all the tithes for their own use. The poor were helpless in the matter of claiming their share of the tithes. It was in the fourteenth century that the abuse of church rates was fully established.

I shall now pass on to the repairs of parish churches. The tithe owners at the present day repair the chancels of their churches out of the tithe rent charges. Is the church the chancel only?

Defence of the Church of England. 173

No. The word "church" includes both nave and chancel. Lyndwode says, "Quod dicit ecclesiæ comprehendit ecclesiam integram, videlicet, navem cum cancello" (*Provinciale*, 53).

Why should the tithe owner repair only the chancel, and not the nave also? Why should he repair the chancel at all? Why should not the parishioners repair the chancel as well as the nave? Why should the parishioners repair any part of the parish church? These questions crop up in dealing with such a matter.

John de Athon, who wrote commentaries in the middle of the fourteenth century on the Constitutions of Otho, a Papal legate that held a national council in London in 1237, informs us that the canon law imposed on the rector the reparation of his church, meaning the nave as well as the chancel. Lord Selborne (p. 153) says that it was at variance with the ecclesiastical and common law of England to throw the burden of the repair of churches upon the tithes. He also quotes the 29th article of the laws of Canute, of A.D. 1018, that "All the people ought of right to assist in repairing the church." Which are we to believe? There is historical evidence that the burden of repairing the parish churches was placed on the parishioners in the thirteenth century, and the abuse of church rates was fully established in the fourteenth century for the following reasons :—

(1.) The heavy exactions of the Court of Rome on the clergy had driven them to the expedient of relieving the pressure on themselves of repairing the churches. (2.) The appropriators so shamefully neglected the repairs of their churches out of the tithes, that the parishioners by their own voluntary contributions kept the roofs and other parts of their parish churches in repairs as a cover and protection to themselves and their families when attending divine service. It was irreverent and indecent in the eyes of the parishioners to see their churches like barns, with the rain coming through the roofs and trickling down the walls, all through the neglect of the appropriators who employed miserably paid vicars to perform the clerical functions in the churches, but took good care to get the greater part of the tithes and offerings for themselves. I have already explained how parliament had to pass laws to protect the interests of the poor and the vicars of such appropriated parishes against the appropriators. The parishioners for their own comfort, decency, and reverence, voluntarily contributed funds to keep their churches in repairs. This purely voluntary act, like the original free-will offering of tithes, became a

Defence of the Church of England. 175

custom, and from a custom it passed into a common right, hence, a common law right, that parishioners should repair their own churches.

Man is a very imitative animal. The rectors who were not appropriators borrowed a leaf from the custom adopted by the parishioners of appropriated parishes, as regards the repairs of their churches. The rectors gradually relieved themselves of the burden of repairing their churches, and placed it on the voluntary contributions of the parishioners. Church rates had their origin in this custom of voluntary contributions. In the fourteenth century church rates were fully established. Then the ecclesiastical courts commenced to compel the parishioners to repair their churches.

I have explained in chapter v., p. 48, how the Norman monks, after the Conquest, introduced the custom of appropriating the tithes and churches to the monastic corporations. I have also shown how the capitular chapters, nuns, and religious military orders *imitated* the practice initiated by the Norman monks. We have, in the case of the repairs of appropriated churches by parishioners, the *imitative* procedure carried out by rectors of parishes which were not appropriated. We observe this custom of repairing the parish churches by the voluntary payments of parishioners, gradually changing into a common right. The burden was removed from the tithe owners to the tithe payers, and the ecclesiastical courts—the great clerical champions—compelled them to keep their churches in repairs. We observe also in the case of tithes, that their payment in England originated in a purely voluntary free-will offering. In course of time, the custom became a common right, and by virtue of this right, people were compelled to pay tithes.

INDEX.

ABEL killed by Cain for tithing evilly, 4
Abraham, first tithe payer, 1
Adam, paid tithes, 3, 166
Alcuin on tithes, 32
Alien priories, 90 ; property seized by Edward I., 101
Althorp, Lord, failed in solving the tithe question, 113
Animadversions on Selden's tithes, 7
Apollo, 3
Apostolical constitutions, 6
Archbishops—Augustin, founder of the Anglo-Saxon Church, 15, 17, 18, 24 ; Egbert of York, canons of, 27, 167 ; Dunstan, 30, 167 ; first Episcopal pluralist, 83 ; Wolsey another great pluralist, 83 ; Howley's statement in "Lords" on church endowments, 76
Athelstan, orders of, to pay tithes, 167
Athon, John de, Commentaries of, 173
Augustin, of Hippo, 27

BARTHOLOMEW, ST, hospital founded and endowed by Henry VIII. ; its tithe endowments, 146, 147
Bedford, Duke, yearly revenue from abbey lands, 107, 162
Bede, Venerable, 14 ; ecclesiastical history, 18

Bellarmine, Cardinal, 6
Benedictine Order, 17
Benefices, number of, in 1831 and 1887, 60
Bishops—Mellitus, 18; Justin, 18 ; bishops ceased to live in common with their clergy, number of, in A.D. 705 in England and Wales, 25 ; Augustin of Hippo, 27 ; Stubbs, 33 ; Sumner of Winchester, questioned in "Lords," the right of Legislature to deal with church property given by individuals to the church "for certain specific purposes," 76 ; Dr Howley stated that these purposes no longer existed, 76 ; Tanner, "Notitia Monastica," monasteries erected from William I. to Henry VI., 89 ; "Commendams," held by bishops, 83 ; Norman bishops first separated episcopal from capitular revenues ; originated capitular separate estates and prebends, 87
Blackstone, Sir William, remarks of, on 15 Richard II., c. 6, 29, 171
Botolph, St, Without, Aldgate, City of London, tithes commuted ; bought by Edward Jeffries Esdaile, 148-150
Brewer, Dr J. S., "Endowments and Establishment of

M

the Church of England," translates "portiones" = Tithes; states that to live by the Gospel, was to live by tithes, 14, 15
"Brief," "The Englishman's B, for his National Church," published by S.P.C.K., its mistakes, 10-13; 68-74, 76, 77 Britain, 16
"Buffers," 121

CAIN killed Abel because he tithed evilly, 4
Caird, Sir James, "Landed Interest," 122, 123
Canon Law, 10; restrained in three ways (by 2 and 3 Edward VI. c. 13), 41, 42
Canute, laws of, 173
Councils—Mascon, 14; Third Lateran, Acts of, against arbitrary appropriations of laymen, 49; Fourth Lateran gave the parson his parochial right to tithes, 51
Cartusians, received property of alien priories, 101
Cathedral Act, A.D. 1840, eight conventual cathedrals, 88
Celibacy of clergy, 30
Chalchyth, Synod of, 33
Chapels of Ease, 20
Charlemagne, made first lay law for payment of tithes, 31
Christian ministers supported by voluntary contributions, 5
Christ Church, Oxford, built and endowed by Wolsey out of confiscated monastic property, 72
Christ Church, City of London, its revenue from tithes, 147
Church Defence, 15
Church of England, was never the Church of Rome, 70
Church in Wales, 134-137

Churches, parish, built by landowners, 20; building society founded, 60; repairs of, 172-176
Commutation Act, 112; some of its leading provisions, 115, 116; how tithe rent charge is calculated; example given, 116, 117; Comptroller of Corn to announce in *London Gazette* after 1st January each year, the average prices of wheat, barley and oats, 117; 80 sect., makes landlords pay the rent charge, 117; landlords contracted themselves out of this section; dishonest farmers refusing to pay rent charge according to agreements, 118, 119; how to prevent evasion of 80 sect. by landlords, 119; dual landlordism created by, 119; lay impropriators and ecclesiastical commissioners always most exacting tithe owners, 120; injustice of rent charge; owners of houses in cities and towns, and of lands in their neighbourhood, let for building purposes, give no support to religion from enhanced value of property, 121, 122; have tithe-owners lost by Commutation Act? answer, 123
Commissioners, report on monasteries, 105
Cottenham, Lord Chancellor, 136
Councils—Third Lateran, 49, 50, 51; Fourth Lateran, 52, 53, 75; Mascon, 14
Curates, perpetual, called vicars, 60

DANES, first appearance in England, plundering, destroying, and murdering, 80

Index.

Daughter Churches, 45
Dionysius Exiger, 6
Domesday Survey, few references to tithes; none for six counties; no parish churches in three counties, 61, 62
Dominicans, condemned for preaching against tithes, 91

EARL OF CHESTER, Charter of, to Chester Monastery; tithes given as alms in it, 94
Ecclesiastical Commissioners, 45; common fund, 73
Egbert, Archbishop, canons of, 27, 167
Emperors — Constantine, 8; Charles V., 14; Charlemagne, 31
Episcopi clerus, 18
Esdaile, Edward Jeffries, and his successors, lay impropriators of St Botolph-Without, Aldgate, London, 148, 149
Exemptions from paying tithes— Templars, Hospitallers, Cistercians, and Premonstratensians, called the four privileged orders, 98, 99; purchasing bulls of exemption stopped, 99; exempted lands given away by Henry VIII. exempted from tithes up to present day, 99, 100
Extraordinary Tithe Redemption Act, principal provisions of, 129, 130

FRIAR CRAB, 14
Friars, Franciscans and Dominicans, poverty their ruling idea, preached tithes were but alms, condemned as heretics, 90-92

GALATIA, Church of, 5

HALLAM, Henry, on Charlemagne's law for payment of tithes, 32
Hercules, 3
House of Commons, petitions of, against canons for payment of tithes; power of canon limited; first victory of, as regards payment of tithes, 66, 68, 102
Hop duty repealed, 128
Howley, Archbishop of Canterbury, statement in the Lords on Church Endowments, 76
IMPROPRIATORS, Lay, meaning of word, 98, 159
Infeudations, Third Lateran Council was the first to condemn them, 97; Henry VIII.'s, 97
Ingulph, his construction of Ethelwulph's charter; Selden doubts his construction, 37
Introduction, xi.-xxvii.
Ireland, 16
Isidore, 14

JACOB, 1
Jewish law on tithes not binding on Christians, 5
Jewish Priests, share of tithes, heave offerings, 2
Johnson, Laws and Canons, 169, 170
Josephus, 12
Jus Parochiale, and Jus Commune, the distinction, 77, 78

KING MELCHIZEDEK, first recorded tithe owner, 1
Kings, Anglo Saxon, Ethelbert of Kent, 17; Offa's grant of tithes, 34, 165-167; Ethelbert of East Angles, murdered, 34; Ethelwulph's Charter, 35-37, 167, 168; Kings who confirmed it, 39

Kings of England, Edgar, 21; his laws on tithes, 44; refounded many monasteries, 83; leading church ideas of, 84; Ethelred the Unready, 28; William I., 30; Henry II., 61; John, 51; Henry V. built and endowed colleges out of confiscated alien priories, 102; Henry VI. founded Eton College and King's, Cambridge, out of the confiscated property of the alien priories, 103; Henry VIII., 97, 103; "Supreme head of the Church of England" appoints commissioners to value benefices, 104, 105; the monks hated him, Henry had his revenge, commission to visit monasteries, report destroyed in Mary's reign; Leigh and Leyton, unscrupulous commissioners, 105; all monasteries with less than £200 a year, dissolved, revenues from same; conditions upon which the property of religious houses were given to the king, 106, 107; lay impropriators, 107; Duke of Bedford, large lay impropriator, Bishoprics created by Henry, 107; executed three abbots, 109; bribes offered to both Houses of Parliament and to the Clergy in order to acquiesce in his spoliation, 109, 110; total revenue received from confiscated monastic properties, 110; his high-handed conduct, 161, 162; Edward VI. and Elizabeth shared in the spoliation of church properties like their father, 108, 161, 162; James I. permitted the clergy to marry, 30

Knights Hospitallers, received lands of Templars, 101.

LAY PATRONAGE, origin of, 22; selling advowsons, traffic in livings, 23
Leigh and Leyton, commissioners to visit monasteries, 105
Legates, first sent to England, 33
Levites received tithes, 2, 3
London, City and Liberties, how citizens originally supported the Christian Churches; tripartite division of their freewill offerings; customary payments, 2s. 6d. in the pound, divided among poor, church, and clergy, 140; Bishop Roger's constitution or "modus," 141; Archbishop Arundell's change of Bishop Roger's modus, 142; 9d. in the pound was the parson's share of the tithes of his parish before the Reformation, 144; tithes of 51 parishes, destroyed by the fire of 1666, regulated by Act of Parliament; provisions of this Act, 145, 146
Lot, 1

MATER ECCLESIA, 18
Market Gardens Act passed on account of action of Vicar of Gulval, 128
Milner on Charlemagne's law for the payment of tithes, 31
Monasteries, 47, 49; monastic tithes of two kinds, 54; number of monasteries in England, A.D. 1215, when their decadence commenced, 75; Glastonbury first British monastery, its first abbot, 80; their advantages, &c., 85, 86; their

number from William I. to Henry VI., 89; Earl of Chester's charter to, 94, 95; dissolution, 101; number dissolved, property, 106, 110; three abbots executed by Henry VIII., 109
"Monasticon," Sir William Dugdale; our greatest storehouse of monastic news, 73
Monks,. Norman; initiated the custom of appropriating tithes and churches to monasteries; capitular bodies, nuns, and other religious houses followed their example, 47-49; English monks passed through three reformations, 84; hostile to Henry VIII., 105

OBLATIONS and Offerings, monthly, 8

PALEY, ARCHDEACON, on tithes, 112
Parishes, number in England and Wales at Reformation, 59
Parochial boundaries commenced, 21; parish system commenced and completed, 53, 75
Parsons' common right to tithes, 52; their duties for tithes, 73
Peel, Sir Robert, Tithe Bill, 114
Phillimore, Sir Robert, 41, 42
Popes—Clement I., 6; Gregory I., 15, 17, 25; Innocent III., 28; commencement of their power in England, and when it reached its zenith, 30; Hildebrand, 30; Adrian I., 33; Alexander III. most energetic in his orders to English archbishops and bishops for the payment of tithes, 60, 61; Pius V., his creed, 74
Prideaux, Dean, Ethelwulph's Charter, 35; his mistaken interpretation of this charter, 167, 168

QUEENS OF ENGLAND, Anne, 2; Mary and Elizabeth, 30; Mary repealed Act of A.D. 1547 which permitted clergy to marry; Elizabeth declined to repeal this Act, but James I. did, and so enabled clergy to marry, 30

REDEMPTION OF TITHES, 124, 125, 151-159; Extraordinary Tithe Redemption Act, 129
Redemption viewed from another point, 157-159; observations on the Redemption scheme, 160-164
Retrospective view of tithes in England, population of England and Wales at different periods and number of acres under cultivation at such periods, 137-139
Roger, Bishop of London; the constitution or modus of, for city of London, for payment of tithes, 141, 142
Russell, Lord John, solved the tithe problem by the Commutation Bill, 114, 115; he said, "Tithes were the property of the nation," 115; was mistaken in his sanguine remarks on the Commutation Act, 131

SELBORNE, EARL OF, his pamphlet, 70, his "Defence of the Church of England against Disestablishment," remarks thereon, 165-173; he ignores grants of tithes by Kings Offa and Ethelwulph, and division of tithes, 165-172; he holds

Index.

that repairs of churches should be made by parishioners and not out of tithes, 173; his various arguments combated, 166-176
Selden, John, history of tithes, 4, 6, 14, 22, 37, 49, 78, 79, 91, 93, 99, 170
Scripture quotations—
  Genesis (xiv. 20), (xxviii. 22), 1;
  Deut. (xiv. 22), 1; Leviticus (xxviii. 30-32), 2; Acts (ii. 44), (iv. 34), 1 Cor. (ix. 13), 15; 1 Cor. (xvi. 1, 2), 5
Smith, Adam, on tithes, 110
Spelman, Sir Henry, 6
Statutes—
  25 Henry I., benefices not to be accepted from laymen without assent of bishop, 50
  15 Rich. II., c. 6, Appropriations, 29, 55, 171, 172
  16 Rich. II., c. 5, Praemunire, 99
  23 Edward I., 63
  17 Edward II., lands of Templars seized and transferred to Knights Hospitallers, 101
  25 Edward III. and 27 Edward III., Provisors, 99
  45 Edward III., trees of twenty years' growth not tithable, 66
  4 Henry IV., c. 12, makes better provision for vicars, 56
  Mortmain Act, A.D. 1297, forbids subjects without king's licence, bequeathing lands, &c., to religious houses, 67
  27 Henry VIII., c. 20, tithes, 110
  27 Henry VIII.,c. 21, London tithes, 143
  27 Henry VIII., caps. 27, 28, dissolving monasteries, 106
  31 Henry VIII., c. 13, lands exempted from tithes to be also exempted when vested in Crown, 100
  32 Henry VIII., c. 7, s. 5, tithes not to be paid by exempted lands, 110
  37 Henry VIII., c. 12, London tithes, 143
  A.D. 1547, Act passed permitting clergy to marry; Mary repealed it, James I. repealed Mary's Act, 30
  2 and 3 Edward VI., cap. 13, personal tithes, 40, 41
  Phillimore shows that this Act restrains the Canon law in three ways, 41
  2 and 3 Edward VI., c. 13, s. 5, barren or waste lands brought into cultivation to pay tithes at end of seven years, 137, 138
  1 Eliz., c. 19, exchanges confiscated rectorial tithes for episcopal lands, 108
  22 and 23 Charles II., c. 15, tithes to fifty-one London churches whose parishes were detroyed by fire, 145
  6 and 7 William IV., c. 71, Commutation Act, 112
  2 and 3 Vict. c. 62, s. 27, orchards exempted from paying extraordinary rent charge, 128
  36 and 37 Vict., c. 42, market gardens, and newly cultivated as such, 129
  42 and 43 Vict. c. 93, Christ Church, City of London, Tithe Act, 147
  42 and 43 Vict. c. 176, City of London Tithes Act, 148
  44 and 45 Vict. c. 197, City of London Tithes, St Botolph-Without, Aldgate, 148

49 and 50 Vict. c. 54, Extraordinary Tithe Redemption Act, 129
Sumner, Bishop of Winchester, in the "Lords" he questioned the right of the Legislature to deal with church property given by individuals for "certain specific purposes," 76; Dr Howley had shown these "certain specific purposes" no longer existed, 76
Synods—Westminster A.D. 1175 and Synod in Northern Province A.D. 1195, both ordered payment of tithes, 61; London A.D. 1295, passed most important canon for payment of tithes, 63; Chalchyth, 33

TANET, Isle of, 17
Tanner, bishop, "notitia monastica," number of monasteries erected from William I. to Henry VI., 89
Templars, lands seized by Act of Parliament, and given to Knights Hospitallers, 101
Tertullian, 10
Tillesley, Dr R., Archdeacon of Rochester, wrote "Animadversions" on Selden's History of Tithes; believed in part of "Apostolical Constitutions," 7, 8; his fiction, 35
Tithes, Abraham paid, 1; Mosaic law for payment of, 1, 2; heathen nations copied Jews in payment of, 3; no order in New Testament for their payment, 5; division of, 8; originally spontaneous offerings, 10; quadripartite and tripartite divisions, 25; arguments for tripartite division in England, 22, 27, 28; Charlemagne made the first lay law for their payment; definition of predial and personal; Scripture in support of personal tithes, 40; "great" and "small," 42; houses not tithable, 43; modus decimandi, 43; parson's common right to, 52; Pope Alexander III.'s energetic orders for their payment, 60; synods which passed canons for their payment, 61, 62, 63; the most important canon for their payment in England, 63; difference between paying tithes and paying rent, rates, and taxes, 69; main object of granting tithes, 70; Fourth Lateran Council ordered tithes to be paid to parochial clergy only, 75; John Wickliffe, Franciscans and Dominicans preached against tithes; their views condemned as heretical, 91-94; Tithes, not due by divine right, 94; Paley and Adam Smith on tithes, 112, 113; Lord Althorp failed in solving tithe question, 113; Sir R. Peel's attempt, 114; Lord Russell's Commutation Bill, 114-125; extraordinary tithes brought into Commutation Act by Lord Russell, 125-129; two statutes declare extraordinary rent charge wrong in principle, 129; redemption of tithes, 124, 125, 151-164; extraordinary tithe redemption Act, 129; tithes in Wales, 134, 135; tithes in City and Liberties of London, 140-150; septennial averages of tithes for fifty years, 133; retrospective view of tithes in England, 137-139; rent charge for

1887, and amounts of redemption and incomes calculated thereon, 155-159; lay impropriators, schools, colleges, &c., redemption and incomes, 159; what should be done with their incomes, 160, 161

VICARS, miserably paid by appropriators, 55, 56; vicars perpetual of 4 Henry IV., c. 12, not to be confounded with "Perpetual Curates," the distinction, 57; abuses arising from incumbent's freehold tenure, parochial autocrat; the remedy, 58, 59; vicars before Reformation not to be confounded with modern vicars, 60; perpetual curates called vicars, 60

WITENAGEMOT, its constitution, 38

Wickliffe, John, opinion of, on tithes, his views condemned as heretical, questioned the pope's supremacy, detested the monks, lashed the parochial clergy, 91-93

Wolsey, built and endowed Christ Church, Oxford, out of the funds of forty suppressed monasteries, 103

Wales, tithes in, 134; church in Wales, 134-137

A Selection
FROM
Mr. Redway's Publications.

GEORGE REDWAY,
15, YORK STREET, COVENT GARDEN, LONDON.
1886.

15, YORK STREET, COVENT GARDEN
LONDON, *September*, 1886.

In large 8vo., uniform with the New " Standard" Edition.
Nearly ready.

Sultan Stork,

AND OTHER STORIES AND PAPERS HITHERTO UNCOLLECTED.

BY

WILLIAM MAKEPEACE THACKERAY.

None of these pieces are included in the two recently published volumes issued by Messrs. SMITH, ELDER, and Co.

With an Appendix containing the Bibliography of THACKERAY (first published in 1880), in a revised and enlarged form.

CONTENTS.

INTRODUCTION.

I. PROSE.

1. **SULTAN STORK**; being the One Thousand and Second Night. By Major G. O' G. GAHAGAN. [1842.]
2. **LITTLE SPITZ.** A Lenten Anecdote. [1841.]
3. **DICKENS IN FRANCE.** An Account of a French dramatic version of "Nicholas Nickleby," performed at a Paris theatre. [1842.]
4. **THE PARTIE FINE.** [1844.]
5. **ARABELLA; or The Moral of the Partie Fine.** [1844.]
6. **CARLYLE'S FRENCH REVOLUTION.** [1837.]
7. **ELIZABETH BROWNRIGGE:** A Tale. [1832.]
8. **AN EXHIBITION GOSSIP.** [1842.]
9. **LETTERS ON THE FINE ARTS.** [1843.]
10. **PARIS CORRESPONDENCE.** [1833.]

II. VERSE.

11. **SATIRICAL VERSES** descriptive of (1) LOUIS PHILIPPE; (2) Mr. BRA-HAM; (3) N. M. ROTHSCHILD, Esq.; (4) A. BUNN; (5) Sir PETER LAURIE (Petrus Laureus). [1833.]
12. **LOVE IN FETTERS.** A Tottenham Court Road Ditty. [1833.]
13. **"DADDY, I'M HUNGRY."** Scene in an Irish Coachmaker's Family. [1843.]

THE BIBLIOGRAPHY OF THACKERAY. A Bibliographical List, arranged in chronological order, of the published Writings in Prose and Verse, and the Sketches and Drawings, of WILLIAM MAKEPEACE THACKERAY (1829-1886). Revised and Enlarged.

GEORGE REDWAY, YORK STREET, COVENT GARDEN.

In crown 8vo., in French grey wrapper. Price 6s.
A few copies on Large Paper. Price 10s. 6d.

The Bibliography of Swinburne;

A BIBLIOGRAPHICAL LIST, ARRANGED IN CHRONOLOGICAL ORDER, OF THE PUBLISHED WRITINGS IN VERSE AND PROSE

OF

ALGERNON CHARLES SWINBURNE

(1857-1884).

This Bibliography commences with the brief-lived *College Magazine*, to which Mr. SWINBURNE was one of the chief contributors when an undergraduate at Oxford in 1857-8. Besides a careful enumeration and description of the first editions of all his separately published volumes and pamphlets in verse and prose, the original appearance is duly noted of every poem, prose article, or letter, contributed to any journal or magazine (*e.g., Once a Week, The Spectator, The Cornhill Magazine, The Morning Star, The Fortnightly Review, The Examiner, The Dark Blue, The Academy, The Athenæum, The Tatler, Belgravia, The Gentleman's Magazine, La République des Lettres, Le Rappel, The Glasgow University Magazine, The Daily Telegraph*, etc., etc.), whether collected or uncollected. Among other entries will be found a remarkable novel, published in instalments, and never issued in a separate form, and several productions in verse not generally known to be from Mr. SWINBURNE's pen. The whole forms a copious, and it is believed approximately complete, record of a remarkable and brilliant literary career, extending already over a quarter of a century.

⁎ *ONLY 250 COPIES PRINTED.*

GEORGE REDWAY, YORK STREET, COVENT GARDEN.

HINTS TO COLLECTORS

OF ORIGINAL EDITIONS OF

THE WORKS OF

Charles Dickens.

BY

CHARLES PLUMPTRE JOHNSON.

Printed on hand-made paper, and bound in vellum.

Crown 8vo., 6s.

The Edition is limited to five hundred and fifty copies, fifty of which are on large paper.

"Enthusiastic admirers of Dickens are greatly beholden to Mr. C P. Johnson for his useful and interesting 'Hints to Collectors of Original Editions of the Works of Charles Dickens' (Redway). The book is a companion to the similar guide to collectors of Thackeray's first editions, is compiled with the like care, and produced with the like finish and taste."—*The Saturday Review.*

"This is a sister volume to the 'Hints to Collectors of First Editions of Thackeray,' which we noticed a month or two ago. The works of Dickens, with a few notable 'Dickensiana,' make up fifty-eight numbers . . . . and Mr. Johnson has further augmented the present volume with a list of thirty-six plays founded on Dickens's works, and another list of twenty-three published portraits of Dickens. As we are unable to detect any slips in his work, we must content ourselves with thanking him for the correctness of his annotations. It is unnecessary to repeat our praise of the elegant *format* of these books. . . . ."—*The Academy.*

"These two elegantly-produced little books, printed on hand-made paper and bound in vellum, should be welcomed by the intending collector of the works of the two authors under treatment, and the more experienced bibliographer will find the verbatim reproductions of the original title-pages not without use. . . . For the purpose of checking the correct numbers of these illustrations, verifying the collations, and detecting possible frauds . . . Mr. Johnson's books are unique. The 'Hints,' moreover, incorporated in his prefaces. . . and the 'Notes' appended to each entry are serviceable, and often shrewd; indeed, the whole labour, evidently one of love, bestowed upon the books is exceptionally accurate and commendable, and we hope to welcome Mr. Johnson at no distant date as a bibliographer of a more pretentious subject."—*Time.*

GEORGE REDWAY, YORK STREET, COVENT GARDEN.

HINTS TO COLLECTORS

OF ORIGINAL EDITIONS OF

THE WORKS OF

William Makepeace Thackeray.

BY

CHARLES PLUMPTRE JOHNSON.

Printed on hand-made paper and bound in vellum. Crown 8vo., 6s.

The Edition is limited to five hundred and fifty copies, twenty-five of which are on large paper.

"... A guide to those who are great admirers of Thackeray, and are collecting first editions of his works. The dainty little volume, bound in parchment and printed on hand-made paper, is very concise and convenient in form; on each page is an exact copy of the title-page of the work mentioned thereon, a collation of pages and illustrations, useful hints on the differences in editions, with other matters indispensable to collectors. .... Altogether it represents a large amount of labour and experience."—*The Spectator.*

"Those who remember with pain having seen the original yellow backs of Thackeray's works knocked to pieces and neglected years ago, may be recommended to read Mr. C. P. Johnson's 'Hints to Collectors.'"—*The Saturday Review.*

"... Mr. Johnson has evidently done his work with so much loving care that we feel entire confidence in his statements. The prices that he has affixed in every case form a valuable feature of the volume, which has been produced in a manner worthy of its subject-matter."—*The Academy.*

"The list of works which Mr. Johnson supplies is likely to be of high interest to Thackeray collectors. His preliminary remarks go beyond this not very narrow circle, and have a value for all collectors of modern works."—*Notes and Queries.*

"... It is choicely printed at the Chiswick Press; and the author, Mr. Charles Plumptre Johnson, treats the subject with evident knowledge and enthusiasm. ... It is not a Thackeray Bibliography, but a careful and minute description of the first issues, with full collations and statement of the probable cost. ... Mr. Johnson addresses collectors, but is in addition a sincere admirer of the greatest satirist of the century."—*Book-Lore.*

"... This genuine contribution to the Bibliography of Thackeray will be invaluable to all collectors of the great novelist's works, and to all who treasure an 'editio princeps' the account here given of the titles and characteristics of the first issues will form a trustworthy guide. ... The special features which will enable the purchaser at once to settle any question of authenticity in copies offered for sale are carefully collated."—*The Publisher's Circular.*

GEORGE REDWAY, YORK STREET, COVENT GARDEN.

Demy 18mo., 200 pages, cloth, uncut. Price 2s.

Wellerisms

FROM

"*Pickwick*" and "*Master Humphrey's Clock.*"

Selected by CHARLES F. RIDEAL.

EDITED, WITH AN INTRODUCTION, BY

CHARLES KENT,

Author of "The Humour and Pathos of Charles Dickens."

"Some write well, but he writes Weller."—*Epigram on Dickens.*

GEORGE REDWAY, YORK STREET, COVENT GARDEN.

In crown 8vo., 2 vols., cloth. Price 6s.

The Valley of Sorek.

BY

GERTRUDE M. GEORGE.

With a Critical Introduction by RICHARD HERNE SHEPHERD.

"There is in the book a high and pure moral and a distinct conception of character. . . . The *dramatis personæ* . . . . are in reality strongly individual, and surprise one with their inconsistencies just as real human beings do. . . . There is something powerful in the way in which the reader is made to feel both the reality and the untrustworthiness of his (the hero's) religious fervour, and the character of the atheist, Graham, is not less strongly and definitely conceived. . . . It is a work that shows imagination and moral insight, and we shall look with much anticipation for another from the same hand."—*Contemporary Review.*

GEORGE REDWAY, YORK STREET, COVENT GARDEN.

FIFTH THOUSAND.

An édition de luxe, in demy 18mo.

Bound in fancy cloth, uncut edges. Price 2s.

Tobacco Talk and Smokers' Gossip.

An Amusing Miscellany of Fact and Anecdote relating to "The Great Plant" in all its Forms and Uses, including a Selection from Nicotian Literature.

"One of the best books of gossip we have met for some time. . . . It is literally crammed full from beginning to end of its 148 pages with well-selected anecdotes, poems, and excerpts from tobacco literature and history."—*Graphic.*

"The smoker should be grateful to the compilers of this pretty little volume. . . . No smoker should be without it, and anti-tobacconists have only to turn over its leaves to be converted."—*Pall Mall Gazette.*

"Something to please smokers ; and non-smokers may be interested in tracing the effect of tobacco—the fatal, fragrant herb—on our literature."—*Literary World.*

GEORGE REDWAY, YORK STREET, COVENT GARDEN.

NEW BOOK BY MISS BAUGHAN.

The Handbook of Physiognomy.

BY

ROSA BAUGHAN.

Demy 8vo., wrapper, Price 1s.

"The merit of her book consists in the admirable clearness of her descriptions of faces. So vivid is the impression produced by them that she is able to dispense with illustrations, the reader using the faces of his acquaintances for that purpose. The classification, too, is good, although the astrological headings may be regarded by the profane as fanciful. Physiognomy may now be scientifically studied by means of composite photography."—*Pall Mall Gazette.*

GEORGE REDWAY, YORK STREET, COVENT GARDEN.

In preparation.
Price to Subscribers, 6s.

The Praise of Ale;

OR,

Songs, Ballads, Epigrams, and Anecdotes relating to

Beer, Malt, and Hops.

Collected and arranged by

W. T. MARCHANT.

CONTENTS.—Introduction.—History.—Carols and Wassail Songs.—Church Ales and Observances.—Whitsun Ales.—Political.—Harvest.—General.—Barley and Malt.—Hops.—Scotch Songs.—Local and Dialect.—Trade Songs.—Oxford Songs.—Ale Wives.—Brewers.—Drinking Clubs and Customs.—Royal and Noble Drinkers.—Black Beer.—Drinking Vessels.—Warm Ale.—Facts, Scraps, and Ana.—Index.

The volume will contain much curious and out-of-the-way information, embracing a short sketch of the rise and progress of the art of brewing in this country; an account of the laws relating to beer, and the statutes against drunkenness; of the manners and customs of "malt worms" and mug-house clubs; and the obsolete phraseology of "toss-pots," such as "super-nagulum," "upsee-freeze," "shoeing horns," and "carousing the hunter's hoop." The author will pay attention to the drinking customs more or less connected with the Church—Whitsun Ales, Bride Ales, Bride Bush, Bride Wain, and the like; the chants of the wassail-bowl, of the Hock Cart, and the Sheepshearing and Harvest Home rejoicings—

"Here's health to the Barley mow, brave boys,
Here's health to the Barley mow"—

and Brazenose songs in honour of the brew for which that college is renowned. Then there are lyrics pertaining to particular sorts and conditions of men, as the songs of the threshers and tinkers, sailors and soldiers, and the clubs, which may be considered as forming a class of themselves. This work will doubtless prove a valuable and pleasant addition to the library of the student of history and lover of poetry.

GEORGE REDWAY, YORK STREET, COVENT GARDEN.

*In crown 8vo., price 6s.
Illustrated with magical signs, and a symbolical frontispiece etched
by Mackaness, from a design by the Author.*

Magic,
WHITE AND BLACK;
Or, The Science of Finite and Infinite Life.

CONTAINING

Practical Hints for Students of Occultism.

BY

FRANZ HARTMANN, M.D.

GEORGE REDWAY, YORK STREET, COVENT GARDEN.

In preparation.
NEW TRANSLATION OF "THE HEPTAMERON."

The Heptameron;
OR,

Tales and Novels of Margaret, Queen of Navarre.

Now first done completely into English prose and verse, from the original French, by ARTHUR MACHEN.

GEORGE REDWAY, YORK STREET, COVENT GARDEN.

Just ready, in small 8vo., cloth, price 5s.

Mountaineering Below the Snow-Line;

Or, the Solitary Pedestrian in Snowdonia and Elsewhere.

BY

M. PATERSON.

WITH ETCHINGS BY MACKANESS.

GEORGE REDWAY, YORK STREET, COVENT GARDEN.

Fourth Edition. With Engraved Frontispiece. In crown 8vo., 5s.

Cosmo de' Medici:

An Historical Tragedy. And other Poems.

BY

RICHARD HENGIST HORNE,

Author of "Orion."

"This tragedy is the work of a poet and not of a playwright. Many of the scenes abound in vigour and tragic intensity. If the structure of the drama challenges comparison with the masterpieces of the Elizabethan stage, it is at least not unworthy of the models which have inspired it."—*Times.*

GEORGE REDWAY, YORK STREET, COVENT GARDEN.

Fcap. 8vo., parchment.

Tamerlane and other Poems.

BY

EDGAR ALLAN POE.

First published at Boston in 1827, and now first republished from a unique copy of the original edition, with a preface by RICHARD HERNE SHEPHERD.

Mr. Swinburne has generously praised "so beautiful and valuable a little volume, full of interest for the admirers of Poe's singular and exquisite genius."

GEORGE REDWAY, YORK STREET, COVENT GARDEN.

Just ready, in demy 8vo., choicely printed, and bound in Japanese parchment. Price 7s. 6d.

Primitive Symbolism

As Illustrated in Phallic Worship; or, The Reproductive Principle.

BY

The late HODDER M. WESTROPP.

With an Introduction by MAJOR-GENERAL FORLONG, Author of "Rivers of Life."

"This work is a *multum in parvo* of the growth and spread of Phallicism, as we commonly call the worship of nature or fertilizing powers. I felt, when solicited to enlarge and illustrate it on the sudden death of the lamented author, that it would be desecration to touch so complete a compendium by one of the most competent and soundest thinkers who have written on this world-wide faith. None knew better or saw more clearly than Mr. Westropp that in this oldest symbolism and worship lay the foundations of all the goodly systems we call religions."—J. G. R. FORLONG.

"A well-selected repertory of facts illustrating this subject, which should be read by all who are interested in the study of the growth of religions."—*Westminster Review.*

GEORGE REDWAY, YORK STREET, COVENT GARDEN.

In large crown 8vo. Price 3s. 6d.

Sithron, the Star Stricken.

Translated (*Ala bereket Allah*) from an ancient Arabic Manuscript.

BY

SALEM BEN UZAIR, of Bassora.

"This very remarkable book, 'Sithron'... is a bold, pungent, audacious satire upon the ancient religious belief of the Jews.... No one can read the book without homage to the force, the tenderness, and the never-failing skill of its writer."—*St. James's Gazette.*

GEORGE REDWAY, YORK STREET, COVENT GARDEN.

THE ONLY PUBLISHED BIOGRAPHY OF JOHN LEECH.

An édition de luxe in demy 18mo. Price 1s.

John Leech,

ARTIST AND HUMOURIST.

A BIOGRAPHICAL SKETCH.

BY

FRED. G. KITTON.

New Edition, revised.

"In the absence of a fuller biography we cordially welcome Mr. Kitton's interesting little sketch."—*Notes and Queries.*

"The multitudinous admirers of the famous artist will find this touching monograph well worth careful reading and preservation."—*Daily Chronicle.*

"The very model of what such a memoir should be."—*Graphic.*

GEORGE REDWAY, YORK STREET, COVENT GARDEN.

Nearly ready, about 500 pages, crown 8vo., cloth. Price 10s. 6d.

The History of the Forty Vezirs;

OR,

The Story of the Forty Morns and Eves.

Written in Turkish by SHEYKH-ZADA, and now done into English by E. J. W. GIBB, M.R.A.S.

The only complete translation of this collection of tales that has hitherto appeared in any European language is that published in German by Dr. Behrnauer in 1851. A complete text of the romance contains eighty subordinate stories, and this is the number given by Behrnauer; but MSS. differ widely in the selection of such tales, and Mr. Gibb has collected one hundred and twelve distinct stories from different versions that have come under his notice. Among these, all of which will appear in the forthcoming volume will be found variants of many widely distributed popular tales.

GEORGE REDWAY, YORK STREET, COVENT GARDEN.

14　　MR. REDWAY'S PUBLICATIONS.

Fourth Edition, newly revised, in demy 8vo., with Illustrative Plates.
Price 1s.

The Handbook of Palmistry,

BY

ROSA BAUGHAN,

AUTHOR OF "INDICATIONS OF CHARACTER IN HANDWRITING."

"It possesses a certain literary interest, for Miss Baughan shows the connection between palmistry and the doctrines of the Kabbala."—*Graphic.*

"Miss Rosa Baughan, for many years known as one of the most expert proficients in this branch of science, has as much claim to consideration as any writer on the subject."—*Sussex Daily News.*

"People who wish to believe in palmistry, or the science of reading character from the marks of the hand," says the *Daily News*, in an article devoted to the discussion of this topic, "will be interested in a handbook of the subject by Miss Baughan, published by Mr. Redway."

GEORGE REDWAY, YORK STREET, COVENT GARDEN.

In 2 vols., cloth, 6s.

The Curate's Wife.

A NOVEL.

BY

J. E. PANTON,

Author of "Sketches in Black and White."
"Less than Kin," etc.

"The author of 'Less Than Kin' has produced in 'The Curate's Wife' a story as powerful and full of genuine human interest as has appeared for some long time past. This tale of 'country life' is realistic in the best sense of the word. Faithful as a photograph in all its minor details, it shows clear insight into character of both the sexes, and under very varied conditions. The gradual transformation of the heroine from a young girl, full of high purposes and enthusiasm, into the hopeless drudge who in despair lays herself down to die, is painted with an almost Zola-like fidelity. Her tyrant, the popular curate, is also a powerful sketch. It is difficult not to think that an expiation worked out in the scene of his misdeeds, with people who pity while they blame him, is insufficient punishment for so contemptible a cur. It would have been, doubtless, more satisfactory had Meta conquered in the unequal contest between her well-meaning inexperience and her husband's brutal self-love, but in real life the chances would be against her, and this clever novel is, above all, an exact picture of certain phases of human nature as it is, and in this lies its chief merit."—*Morning Post, May 19th, 1886.*

GEORGE REDWAY, YORK STREET, COVENT GARDEN.

NEW NOVEL BY MR. A. P. SINNETT,
Author of " Karma," etc.

Published at 21s. Now offered at 10s. 6d. In 2 vols., crown 8vo., cloth.

United.

BY

A. P. SINNETT.

"Mr. Sinnett's previous works on 'Esoteric Buddhism' and 'The Occult World' in some way prepare the reader for the marvellous psychological phenomena with which the present volumes abound, and which cannot fail to have an irresistible charm for all those who love the byeways of speculation."—*Literary World.*

"There is, nevertheless, a weird attractiveness about UNITED which makes even the non-believer in theosophy loth to put down the book when once he has taken it up; while to the lovers of occult phenomena it will prove irresistibly fascinating."—*Literary World.*

"Literary ability is evident throughout the book."—*St. James's Gazette.*

"Mr. Sinnett has produced a novel, turning on psychic, mesmeric, and magnetic causes operating on English men and women of ordinary and very extraordinary types, and he has succeeded in making it of special interest for spiritualists, and readable by common people."—*The Lady.*

"It is even doubtful whether Mr. Sinnett will win one genuine convert to occultism by UNITED; but those who are occult already will take his powerful romance to their hearts; will pour out libations before him, and loudly cry 'Well done!'"—*Court and Society Review.*

"Over this thrice-silly subject the author has expended some most excellent writing, ideas that equal in breadth and strength some of those of our best writers, pure English, and undeniable grammar."—*The Whitehall Review.*

GEORGE REDWAY, YORK STREET, COVENT GARDEN.

Just published, 32 pages, wrapper. Price 1s.

The New Illumination.

BY

EDWARD MAITLAND,

AUTHOR OF "THE PILGRIM AND THE SHRINE."

GEORGE REDWAY, YORK STREET, COVENT GARDEN.

MR. REDWAY'S PUBLICATIONS.

In Preparation.

The Life and the Substance of the Teachings of
Philipp Theophrastus, Bombast of Hohenheim,

KNOWN BY THE NAME OF

Paracelsus,

An Adept of the Secret Science.

Containing his essential doctrines in regard to Cosmology, Pneumatology, Magic, Medicine, Alchemy, Theosophy, and Philosophy, and some important secrets, such as the preparation of the true Elixir of Life, the Electro-Magicon, the generation of Homunculi, the nature of Elemental Spirits, etc.

Extracted and translated from his extensive works and from some unpublished Manuscripts, and supplied with Annotations, by

F. HARTMANN, M.D.,

AUTHOR OF "MAGIC," ETC.

GEORGE REDWAY, YORK STREET, COVENT GARDEN.

---

64 *pp.*, 8*vo.*, *wrapper.* Price 1*s.* 6*d.*

THE

"Occult World Phenomena,"

AND

The Society for Psychical Research.

BY

A. P. SINNETT,

AUTHOR OF "THE OCCULT WORLD," "ESOTERIC BUDDHISM," ETC.

With a Protest by MADAME BLAVATSKY.

"An interesting addition to the fast-expanding literature of Theosophy."—*Literary World.*
"All who are interested in Theosophy should read it."—*Glasgow Herald.*
"Mr. Sinnett scores some points against his adversary, and his pamphlet is to be followed by some memoirs of Madame Blavatsky, which may contain further refutations. Madame Blavatsky herself appends to the pamphlet a brief and indignant denial of the grave charges which have been made against her."—*Graphic.*

GEORGE REDWAY, YORK STREET, COVENT GARDEN.

In crown 8vo., parchment. Price 3s. 6d.

The Anatomy of Tobacco;

Or, Smoking Methodised, Divided, and Considered after a New Fashion.

BY

LEOLINUS SILURIENSIS.

"A very clever and amusing parody of the metaphysical treatises once in fashion. Every smoker will be pleased with this volume."—*Notes and Queries.*

"We have here a most excellent piece of fooling, evidently from a University pen. . . . contains some very clever burlesques of classical modes of writing, and a delicious parody of scholastic logic."—*Literary World.*

"A delightful mock essay on the exoteric philosophy of the pipe and the pipe bowl . . . . reminding one alternately of 'Melancholy' Burton and Herr Teufelsdröch, and implying vast reading and out-of-the-way culture on the part of the author."—*Bookseller.*

GEORGE REDWAY, YORK STREET, COVENT GARDEN.

In demy 8vo., with Illustrative Plates. Price 1s. 6d.

Chirognomancy;

Or, Indications of Temperament and Aptitudes Manifested by the Form and Texture of the Thumb and Fingers.

BY

ROSA BAUGHAN.

"Miss Baughan has already established her fame as a writer upon occult subjects, and what she has to say is so very clear and so easily verified that it comes with the weight of authority."—*Lady's Pictorial.*

"Ingenious and not uninteresting."—*The Queen.*

GEORGE REDWAY, YORK STREET, COVENT GARDEN.

MR. REDWAY'S PUBLICATIONS.

Annual subscription, payable in advance, post free, 5s.

The East Anglian;
OR,
Notes and Queries

ON SUBJECTS CONNECTED WITH THE COUNTIES OF SUFFOLK, CAMBRIDGE, ESSEX, AND NORFOLK.

Issued Monthly.

EDITED BY THE

Rev. C. H. EVELYN WHITE, F.R.Hist.S., Ipswich,

HONORARY SECRETARY OF THE SUFFOLK INSTITUTE OF ARCHÆOLOGY AND NATURAL HISTORY.

"Antiquities are history defaced, or remnants that have escaped the shipwreck of time .... wrecks of history wherein the memory of things is almost lost; or such particulars as industrious persons, with exact and scrupulous diligence can anyway collect from genealogies, calendars, titles, inscriptions, monuments, coins, names, etymologies, proverbs, traditions, archives, instruments, fragments of private and public history, scattered passages, of books no way historical, etc., by which means something is recovered from the deluge of time..... In this imperfect history no deficiency need be noted, it being of its own nature imperfect."—*Lord Bacon, Advancement of Learning.*

GEORGE REDWAY, YORK STREET, COVENT GARDEN.

In imperial 16mo., Dutch paper, cloth extra.   Price 2s. 6d.

The Rueing of Gudrun,
And other Poems.

BY THE

Hon. Mrs. GREVILLE-NUGENT.

"It is clear from many exquisite passages that Mrs. Nugent, if she were so minded and in earnest, might be a real poetess."—*Daily Telegraph.*

"The writer touches the various chords of her lyre with no inexperienced hand."—*Morning Post.*

"Mrs. Greville-Nugent has succeeded very fairly well with her villanelles and rondeaux, her triolets and sestines, her ballades and chants royal."—*St. James's Gazette.*

"Where she shows herself at her best is in the French forms of verse, which exactly suit her talent."—*The Times.*

GEORGE REDWAY, YORK STREET, COVENT GARDEN.

In preparation.

THE PLAYS OF GEORGE COLMAN THE YOUNGER.

The Comedies and Farces

OF

GEORGE COLMAN THE YOUNGER.

Now first collected and carefully reprinted from the Original Editions, with Annotations and Critical and Bibliographical Preface,

BY

RICHARD HERNE SHEPHERD.

In Two Volumes.

"Mr. R. H. Shepherd is engaged in collecting and reprinting, with a critical and biographical introduction and annotations, the dramatic works of George Colman the younger, which will shortly be published in two volumes by Mr. Redway, of York Street. Most of them were issued in Colman's lifetime in pamphlet form, but many have, nevertheless, become scarce, and of those which, like the 'Heir-at-Law,' 'John Bull,' and 'The Poor Gentleman,' have held the stage, the text has become more or less corrupted. Considering the great popularity of Colman's plays, the spirit and humour of their scenes, and their association with the names of great actors in the past, it is a curious fact that Mr. Shepherd's publication, though it appears more than a century after the production of the earliest of Colman's pieces on the stage, will be the first collected edition. It will comprise, of course, the suppressed preface to 'The Iron Chest,' in which Colman made his famous personal attack upon John Kemble."—*Daily News.*

GEORGE REDWAY, YORK STREET, COVENT GARDEN.

An édition de luxe, in demy 18mo. Price 1s.

Confessions of an English Hachish Eater.

"There is a sort of bizarre attraction in this fantastic little book, with its weird, unhealthy imaginations."—*Whitehall Review.*

"Imagination or some other faculty plays marvellous freaks in this little book."—*Lloyd's Weekly.*

"A charmingly written and not less charmingly printed little volume. The anonymous author describes his experiences in language which for picturesqueness is worthy to rank with De Quincey's celebrated sketch of the English Opium Eater."—*Lincolnshire Chronicle.*

"A weird little book. . . . The author seems to have been delighted with his dreams, and . . . . carefully explains how hachish may be made from the resin of the common hemp plant."—*Daily Chronicle.*

"To be added to the literature of what is, after all, a very undesirable subject. Weak minds may generate a morbid curiosity if stimulated in this direction."—*Bradford Observer.*

"The stories told by our author have a decidedly Oriental flavour, and we would not be surprised if some foolish individuals did endeavour to procure some of the drug, with a view to experience the sensation described by the writer of this clever brochure."—*Edinburgh Courant.*

GEORGE REDWAY, YORK STREET, COVENT GARDEN.

Monthly, One Shilling.

Walford's Antiquarian :

A Magazine and Bibliographical Review.

EDITED BY

EDWARD WALFORD, M.A.

*** *Volumes I. to IX., Now Ready, price 8s. 6d. each.*

"The excellent archæological monthly."—*Cassell's Art and Literature.*

"This magazine is dear to the hearts of the lovers of antiquities. The meetings of the various learned societies are also described. . . . and a number of articles of both antiquarian and bibliographical interest."—*Nonconformist.*

"There is not much in *Walford's Antiquarian* that any connoisseur in literary curiosities would care to pass over."—*St. James's Gazette.*

GEORGE REDWAY, YORK STREET, COVENT GARDEN.

Monthly, 2s.; Yearly Subscription, 20s.

The Theosophist:

A Magazine of Oriental Philosophy, Art, Literature and Occultism.

CONDUCTED BY

H. P. BLAVATSKY.

Vols. I. to VII. Now Ready.

"Theosophy has suddenly risen to importance. . . . The movement implied by the term Theosophy is one that cannot be adequately explained in a few words . . . those interested in the movement, which is not to be confounded with spiritualism, will find means of gratifying their curiosity by procuring the back numbers of *The Theosophist* and a very remarkable book called 'Isis Unveiled,' by Madame Blavatsky."—*Literary World.*

GEORGE REDWAY, YORK STREET, COVENT GARDEN.

NEW WORK BY JOHN H. INGRAM.

The Raven.

BY

EDGAR ALLAN POE.

With Historical and Literary Commentary. By JOHN H. INGRAM.

Crown 8vo., parchment, gilt top, uncut, price 6s.

"This is an interesting monograph on Poe's famous poem. First comes the poet's own account of the genesis of the poem, with a criticism, in which Mr. Ingram declines, very properly, we think, to accept the history as entirely genuine. Much curious information is collected in this essay. Then follows the poem itself, with the various readings, and then its after-history; and after these 'Isadore,' by Albert Pike, a composition which undoubtedly suggested the idea of 'The Raven' to its author. Several translations are given, two in French, one in prose, the other in rhymed verse; besides extracts from others, two in German and one in Latin. But perhaps the most interesting chapter in the book is that on the 'Fabrications.'"—*The Spectator.*

"There is no more reliable authority on the subject of Edgar Allan Poe than Mr. John H. Ingram . . . the volume is well printed and tastefully bound in spotless vellum, and will prove to be a work of the greatest interest to all students of English and American literature."—*The Publishers' Circular.*

GEORGE REDWAY, YORK STREET, COVENT GARDEN.

Now ready, at all Booksellers', and at Smith's Railway Bookstalls.
Popular Edition, price 2s. 6d.

Burma:

As it Was, As it Is, and As it Will be.

BY

J. G. SCOTT.

Crown 8vo., cloth.

"Before going to help to govern them, Mr. Scott has once more written on the Burmese . . . Mr. Scott claims to have covered the whole ground, to show Burma as it was, is, and will be; and as there is nobody competent to criticise him except himself, we shall not presume to say how far he has succeeded. What, however, may be asserted with absolute confidence is, that he has written a bright, readable, and useful book."—*Saturday Review*, March 27.

"Very lively and readable."—*Pall Mall Gazette.*

"The author knows what he writes about."—*St. Stephen's Review.*

"There is a good deal of curious reading in the book."—*Literary World.*

"The book is amusing and instructing, and Mr. George Redway, the publisher, will have done the public and himself a service."—*Court Journal.*

"The print is clear, and the binding in excellent taste."—*Bookseller.*

"Evidently full of genuine information."—*Society.*

"A handy guide to Burma, as readable as it is accurate."—*Globe.*

"Mr. Scott should have called this volume 'A book for Members of Parliament.'"—*London and China Telegraph.*

"The sketch of Burmese cosmogony and mythology is very interesting."—*Nature.*

"A competent historian. He sketches Burma and the Burmese with minute fidelity."—*Daily Chronicle.*

"Probably no Englishman knows Burma better than Mr. J. G. Scott."—*Contemporary Review.*

"An excellent description both of land and people."—*Contemporary Review.*

"Most interesting."—*St. James's Gazette.*

"Shway Yoe is a graphic writer . . . no one can supply this information better than Mr. Scott."—*Asiatic Quarterly Review.*

GEORGE REDWAY, YORK STREET, COVENT GARDEN.

Just published, handsomely printed and tastefully bound, 436 *pages, large crown* 8vo., *cloth extra,* 7s. 6d.

Essays in the Study of Folk-Songs.

BY

THE COUNTESS EVELYN MARTINENGO-CESARESCO.

"A pleasant volume on a pleasant topic. . . . The Countess, with her sincere enthusiasm for what is simple, passionate, and sensuous in folk-song, and with her lucid and unaffected style, well understands the mode in which the educated collector should approach the shy singers or story-tellers of Europe. . . . Her introduction is perhaps, to the scientific student of popular culture, the best part of her book. . . . Next to her introduction, perhaps her article on 'Death in Folk-Poetry' is the most serviceable essay in the volume. . . . 'Folk Lullabies' is perhaps the most pleasant of the remaining essays in the admirable volume, a volume remarkable for knowledge, sympathy, and good taste."—Extracts from a page notice in the *Saturday Review*, April 24, 1886.

"This is a very delightful book, full of information and thoughtful suggestions. It deals principally with the Folk-songs of Southern peoples, Venetian, Sicilian, Armenian, Provence, and Greek Songs of Calabria, but there are several essays devoted to the general characteristics of Folk-Poetry, such as the influence of Nature, the Inspiration of Death, the idea of fate, the numerous songs connected with the rites of May, Folk-Lullabies, and Folk-Dirges. There is also an interesting essay on what is called the White Paternoster, and Children's Rhyming Prayers. This is one of the most valuable, and certainly one of the most interesting, books which has been written on a subject which has of late years been exciting an ever-increasing attention, and which involves many important problems connected with the early history of the human race."—*Standard*.

"'Folk-Songs,' traditional popular ballads, are as tempting to me as King Charles's head to Mr. Dick. But interesting as the topic of the origin and diffusion and literary merit of these poems may be—poems much the same in all European countries—they are rather caviare to the general. The Countess Martinengo-Cesaresco is, or should be, a well-known authority among special students of this branch of literature, to whom I heartily commend her 'Essays in the Study of Folk-Songs.' The Countess is, perhaps, most familiar with Southern *volkslieder*, as of Greece, Italy, and Sicily. Her book is a treasure-house of Folk-lore of various kinds, and the matter is handled with much poetic appreciation and a good deal of learning."—*Daily News*.

"A kind of popular introduction to the study of Folk-lore."—*St. James's Gazette*.

GEORGE REDWAY, YORK STREET, COVENT GARDEN.

EBENEZER JONES'S POEMS.

In post 8vo., cloth, old style. Price 5s.

Studies of Sensation and Event.

Poems by EBENEZER JONES.
Edited, Prefaced, and Annotated by RICHARD HERNE SHEPHERD.
With Memorial Notices of the Author by SUMNER JONES
and W. J. LINTON.
A new Edition. With Photographic Portrait of the Poet.

"This remarkable poet affords nearly the most striking instance of neglected genius in our modern school of poetry. His poems are full of vivid disorderly power."—D. G. ROSSETTI.

GEORGE REDWAY, YORK STREET, COVENT GARDEN.

In demy 8vo., elegantly printed on Dutch hand-made paper, and bound in parchment-paper cover. Price 1s.

The Scope and Charm of Antiquarian Study.

BY
JOHN BATTY, F.R.Hist.S.,
MEMBER OF THE YORKSHIRE ARCHÆOLOGICAL AND TOPOGRAPHICAL
ASSOCIATION.

"It forms a useful and entertaining guide to a beginner in historical researches."—*Notes and Queries.*

"The author has laid it before the public in a most inviting, intelligent, and intelligible form, and offers every incentive to the study in every department, including Ancient Records, Manorial Court-Rolls, Heraldry, Painted Glass, Mural Paintings, Pottery, Church Bells, Numismatics, Folk-Lore, etc., to each of which the attention of the student is directed. The pamphlet is printed on a beautiful modern antique paper, appropriate to the subject of the work."—*Brighton Examiner.*

"Mr. Batty, who is one of those folks Mr. Dobson styles 'gleaners after time,' has clearly and concisely summed up, in the space of a few pages, all the various objects which may legitimately be considered to come within the scope of antiquarian study."—*Academy.*

GEORGE REDWAY, YORK STREET, COVENT GARDEN.

A few large-paper copies, with India proof portrait, in imperial 8vo., parchment. Price 7s. 6d.

An Essay on the Genius of George Cruikshank.

BY

"THETA" (WILLIAM MAKEPEACE THACKERAY).

With all the Original Woodcut Illustrations, a New Portrait of CRUIKSHANK, etched by PAILTHORPE, and a Prefatory Note on THACKERAY AS AN ART CRITIC, by W. E. CHURCH, Secretary of the Urban Club.

"Thackeray's essay 'On the Genius of George Cruikshank,' reprinted from the *Westminster Review*, is a piece of work well calculated to drive a critic of these days to despair. How inimitable is its touch! At once familiar and elegant, serious and humorous, enthusiastically appreciative, and yet just and clear-sighted; but, above all, what the French call *personnel*. It is not the impersonnel reviewer who is going through his paces . . . it is Thackeray talking to us as few can talk—talking with apparent carelessness, even ramblingly, but never losing the thread of his discourse or saying a word too much, nor ever missing a point which may help to elucidate his subject or enhance the charm of his essay. . . . Mr. W. E. Church's prefatory note on 'Thackeray as an Art Critic' is interesting and carefully compiled."—*Westminster Review*, Jan. 15th.

"As the original copy of the *Westminster* is now excessively rare, this reissue will, no doubt, be welcomed by collectors."—*Birmingham Daily Mail*.

"Not only on account of the author, but of the object, we must welcome most cordially this production. Every bookman knows Thackeray, and will be glad to have this production of his which deals with art criticism—a subject so peculiarly Thackeray's own."—*The Antiquary*.

"It was a pleasant and not untimely act to reprint this well-known delightful essay. . . . the artist could have found no other commentator so sympathetic and discriminating. . . . The new portrait of Cruikshank by F. W. Pailthorpe is a clear, firm etching."—*The Artist*.

GEORGE REDWAY, YORK STREET, COVENT GARDEN

Edition limited to 500 copies, handsomely printed on antique paper and tastefully bound. Price 7s. 6d.

THE ASTROLOGER'S GUIDE.

Anima Astrologiae;

OR, A

Guide for Astrologers.

Being the One Hundred and Forty-six Considerations of the Astrologer, GUIDO BONATUS, translated from the Latin by Henry Coley, together with the choicest Aphorisms of the Seven Segments of JEROM CARDAN, of Milan, edited by William Lilly (1675); now first republished from the original edition with Notes and Preface

BY

WILLIAM CHARLES ELDON SERJEANT,

"Mr. Serjeant deserves the thanks of all who are interested in astrology for rescuing this important work from oblivion. . . . The growing interest in mystical science will lead to a revival of astrological study, and advanced students will find this book an indispensable addition to their libraries. The book is well got up and printed."—*Theosophist.*

GEORGE REDWAY, YORK STREET, COVENT GARDEN.

In the Press.

Incidents in the Life

OF

Madame Blavatsky,

Compiled from Information supplied by her Relatives and Friends,

AND EDITED BY

A. P. SINNETT.

With a Portrait reproduced from an Original Painting by HERMANN SCHMIECHEN.

GEORGE REDWAY, YORK STREET, COVENT GARDEN.

MR. REDWAY'S PUBLICATIONS. 27

*To be published shortly, handsomely printed and bound in one vol.
Small demy 8vo., price 10s. 6d.*

The Kabala Denudata

(Translated into English),

CONTAINING THE FOLLOWING BOOKS OF THE ZOHAR:—

1. *The Book of Concealed Mystery.*
2. *The Greater Holy Assembly.*
3. *The Lesser Holy Assembly.*

Collated with the original Hebrew and the Latin text of Knorr de Rosenroth's "Kabala Denudata,"

BY

S. LIDDELL MACGREGOR MATHERS.

GEORGE REDWAY, YORK STREET, COVENT GARDEN.

Nearly ready.   Price 1s.

Low Down.

Wayside Thoughts in Ballad and other Verse.

BY

TWO TRAMPS.

"This is a collection of short pieces, most of which can fairly be considered poetry—no slight merit, as verse runs just now. Some of the pieces are singularly pathetic and mournful; others, though in serious guise, are permeated by quaint humour; and all of them are of considerable merit. From the variety and excellence of the contents of this bundle of poetical effusions, it is likely to attract a great number of readers, and many passages in it are particularly suitable for recitation."—*Army and Navy Gazette*, Aug. 14, 1886.

"But 'Low Down,' as it is called, has the distinction of being multicoloured, each sheet of eight pages consisting of paper of a special hue. To turn over the leaves is, in fact, to enjoy a sort of kaleidoscopic effect, a glimpse of a literary rainbow. Moreover, to complete the peculiarity of the thing, the various poems are printed, apparently at haphazard, in large or small type, as the case may be. There are those, perhaps, who would take such jokes too seriously, and bring them solemnly to the bar of taste, there to be as solemnly condemned. But that is scarcely the right spirit in which to regard them. There is room in life for the quaint and curious as well as for the neat and elegant."—*The Globe.*

GEORGE REDWAY, YORK STREET, COVENT GARDEN.

In crown 8vo., cloth. Price 7s. 6d.

Theosophy, Religion, and Occult Science.

BY

HENRY S. OLCOTT,

PRESIDENT OF THE THEOSOPHICAL SOCIETY.

WITH GLOSSARY OF INDIAN TERMS AND INDEX.

"This book, to which we can only allot an amount of space quite incommensurate with its intrinsic interest, is one that will appeal to the prepared student rather than to the general reader. To anyone who has previously made the acquaintance of such books as Mr. Sinnett's 'Occult World,' and 'Esoteric Buddhism,' or has in other ways familiarised himself with the doctrines of the so-called Theosophical Society or Brotherhood, these lectures of Colonel Olcott's will be rich in interest and suggestiveness. The American officer is a person of undoubted social position and unblemished personal reputation, and his main object is not to secure belief in the reality of any 'phenomena,' not to win a barren reputation for himself as a thaumaturgist or wonderworker, but to win acceptance for one of the oldest philosophies of nature and human life—a philosophy to which of late years the thinkers of the West have been turning with noteworthy curiosity and interest. Of course, should the genuineness of the phenomena in question be satisfactorily established, there would undoubtedly be proof that the Eastern sages to whom Colonel Olcott bears witness do possess a knowledge of the laws of the physical universe far wider and more intimate than that which has been laboriously acquired by the inductive science of the West; but the theosophy expounded in this volume is at once a theology, a metaphysic, and a sociology, in which mere marvels, as such, occupy a quite subordinate and unimportant position. We cannot now discuss its claims, and we will not pronounce any opinion upon them; we will only say that Colonel Olcott's volume deserves and will repay the study of all readers for whom the byeways of speculation have an irresistible charm."—*Manchester Examiner*.

GEORGE REDWAY, YORK STREET, COVENT GARDEN.

Post free, price 3d.

The Literature of Occultism and Archæology.

Being a Catalogue of Books ON SALE relating to

Ancient Worships.
Astrology.
Alchemy.
Animal Magnetism.
Anthropology.
Arabic.
Assassins.
Antiquities.
Ancient History.
Behmen and the Mystics.
Buddhism.
Clairvoyance.
Cabeiri.
China.
Coins.
Druids.
Dreams and Visions.
Divination.
Divining Rod.
Demonology.
Ethnology.
Egypt.
Fascination.
Flagellants.
Freemasonry.
Folk-Lore.
Gnostics.
Gems.
Ghosts.
Hindus.
Hieroglyphics and Secret Writing.
Herbals.
Hermetic.
India and the Hindus.
Kabbala.
Koran.
Miracles.
Mirabilaries.

Magic and Magicians.
Mysteries.
Mithraic Worship
Mesmerism.
Mythology.
Metaphysics.
Mysticism.
Neo-platonism.
Orientalia.
Obelisks.
Oracles.
Occult Sciences.
Philology.
Persian.
Parsees.
Philosophy.
Physiognomy.
Palmistry and Handwriting.
Phrenology.
Psychoneurology.
Psychometry.
Prophets.
Rosicrucians.
Round Towers.
Rabbinical.
Spiritualism.
Skeptics. Jesuits, Christians and Quakers.
Sibylls.
Symbolism.
Serpent Worship.
Secret Societies.
Somnambulism.
Travels.
Tombs.
Theosophical.
Theology and Criticism.
Witchcraft.

GEORGE REDWAY, YORK STREET, COVENT GARDEN.

Quarterly, 1s. 6d. Annual subscription, 5s.

Northamptonshire Notes and Queries.

An illustrated quarterly Journal devoted to the Antiquities, Family History, Traditions, Parochial Records, Folk-Lore, Ancient Customs, etc., of the County.

EDITED BY

The Rev. W. D. SWEETING, M.A.

GEORGE REDWAY, YORK STREET, COVENT GARDEN.

The Mysteries of Magic;

BEING THE SUBSTANCE OF

The Writings of "Eliphas Levi"

(ALPHONSE LOUIS CONSTANT).

BY

ARTHUR EDWARD WAITE.

GEORGE REDWAY, YORK STREET, COVENT GARDEN.

In demy 8vo., wrappered, uncut for binding, with Extra Portrait. Price 5s.

"Phiz" (Hablot Knight Browne):

A Memoir; including a Selection from his Correspondence and Notes on his Principal Works. By FRED. G. KITTON.

With a Portrait and numerous Illustrations.

☞ *A few copies only remain.*

GEORGE REDWAY, YORK STREET, COVENT GARDEN.

One vol., crown 8vo., 400 pages. Price 6s.

A Regular Pickle:

How He Sowed his Wild Oats.

BY

HENRY W. NESFIELD.

"Mr. Nesfield's name as an author is established on such a pleasantly sound foundation that it is a recognised fact that, in taking up a book written by him, the reader is in for a delightful half-hour, during which his risible and humorous faculties will be pleasantly stimulated. The history of young Archibald Highton Tregauntly, whose fortunes we follow from the cradle to when experience is just beginning to teach him a few wholesome lessons, is as smart and brisk as it is possible to be."—*Whitehall Review.*

"It will be matter for regret if the brisk and lively style of Mr. Nesfield, who at times reminds us of Lever, should blind people to the downright wickedness of such a perverted career as is here described."—*Daily Chronicle.*

GEORGE REDWAY, YORK STREET, COVENT GARDEN.

In post 8vo., with numerous plates coloured by hand. Price 7s. 6d.

Geometrical Psychology;

OR,

The Science of Representation.

Being the Theories and Diagrams of B. W. BETTS.

EXPLAINED BY

LOUISA S. COOK.

"His attempt (B. W. Betts') seems to have taken a similar direction to that of George Boole in logic, with the difference that, whereas Boole's expression of the Laws of Thought is algebraic, Betts expresses mind-growth geometrically; that is to say, his growth-formulæ are expressed in numerical series, of which each can be pictured to the eye in a corresponding curve. When the series are thus represented, they are found to resemble the forms of leaves and flowers."—*Extract from "Symbolic Methods of Study," by Mary Boole.*

GEORGE REDWAY, YORK STREET, COVENT GARDEN.

NEW REALISTIC NOVEL.

620 *pages, handsomely bound.* *Price* 6s.

Leicester :

AN AUTOBIOGRAPHY.

BY

FRANCIS W. L. ADAMS.

"Even M. Zola and Mr. George Moore would find it hard to beat Mr. Adams's description of Rosy's death. The grimly minute narrative of Leicester's schoolboy troubles and of his attempt to get a living when he is discarded by his guardian is, too, of such a character as to make one regret that Mr. Adams had not put to better use his undoubted, though undisciplined, powers."—*The Academy.*

"There is unquestionable power in 'Leicester.'"—*The Athenæum.*

GEORGE REDWAY, YORK STREET, COVENT GARDEN.

In post 4to. *Illustrated with Engravings on Wood.*

ASTROLOGY THEOLOGIZED.

The Spiritual Hermeneutics of Astrology and Holy Writ.

BEING

A Treatise upon the Influence of the Stars on Man, and on the Art of Ruling them by the Law of Grace.

REPRINTED FROM THE ORIGINAL OF 1649.

With a Prefatory Essay on Bible Hermeneutics.

BY

ANNA KINGSFORD

(Doctor of Medicine of the Paris Faculty).

GEORGE REDWAY, YORK STREET, COVENT GARDEN.

Small 4to., with Illustrations, bound in vegetable parchment.
Price 10s. 6d.

THE
Virgin of the World.

BY HERMES MERCURIUS TRISMEGISTUS.

A Treatise on INITIATIONS, or ASCLEPIOS; the DEFINITIONS of ASCLEPIOS; FRAGMENTS of the WRITINGS of HERMES.

TRANSLATED AND EDITED BY THE AUTHORS OF "THE PERFECT WAY."

With an Introduction to "The Virgin of the World" by A. K., and an Essay on "The Hermetic Books" by E. M.

"It will be a most interesting study for every occultist to compare the doctrines of the ancient Hermetic philosophy with the teaching of the Vedantic and Buddhist systems of religious thought. The famous books of Hermes seem to occupy, with reference to the Egyptian religion, the same position which the Upanishads occupy in Aryan religious literature."—*The Theosophist*, November, 1885.

GEORGE REDWAY, YORK STREET, COVENT GARDEN.

The Path:

A Magazine devoted to the Brotherhood of Humanity, Theosophy in America, and the Study of Occult Science, Philosophy, and Aryan Literature.

EDITED BY

WILLIAM Q. JUDGE.

(Published under the auspices of The Aryan Theosophical Society of New York.)

Monthly. Subscription, 10s. per annum.

GEORGE REDWAY, YORK STREET, COVENT GARDEN.

In large crown 8vo.   In preparation.

Sea Songs and River Rhymes.

A SELECTION OF ENGLISH VERSE, FROM CHAUCER TO SWINBURNE.

EDITED BY

Mrs. DAVENPORT ADAMS.

With Etchings by Mackaness.

This is a Collection of Poems and Passages by English Writers on the subject of the Sea and Rivers, and covers the whole of the ground between Spenser and Tennyson. It includes numerous copyright Poems, for the reproduction of which the author and publishers have given their permission.

"Mrs. W. Davenport Adams, who has produced many charming volumes of verse, has nearly ready 'Sea Songs and River Rhymes.' Mrs. Adams is sure to prepare an interesting work, for she displays considerable industry, coupled with sound scholarship and a cultivated taste."—*Wakefield Free Press.*

GEORGE REDWAY, YORK STREET, COVENT GARDEN.

NEWLY-DISCOVERED POEM BY CHARLES LAMB.

Beauty and the Beast;

OR,

A Rough Outside with a Gentle Heart.

By CHARLES LAMB. Now first reprinted from the Original Edition of 1811, with Preface and Notes

BY

RICHARD HERNE SHEPHERD.

Only 100 Copies printed.

Fcap. 8vo., printed on handsome paper at the Chiswick Press, and bound in parchment by Burn to form a companion volume to "Tamerlane." Price 10s. 6d.

EORGE REDWAY, YORK STREET, COVENT GARDEN.

In small 8vo., handsomely printed on antique paper, and tastefully bound. Price 2s. 6d.

Pope Joan

(THE FEMALE POPE).

A Historical Study. Translated from the Greek of Emmanuel Rhoïdis, with Preface by

CHARLES HASTINGS COLLETTE.

"When Dr. Döllinger wrote to the effect that 'the subject of Pope Joan has not yet lost interest,' he said no more than the truth. The probability is that the topic will always have its attractions for the lovers of the curiosities of history. Mr. Baring-Gould has declared that 'the whole story of Pope Joan is fabulous, and rests on not a single historical foundation;' but others are not so firmly convinced in the matter, and at all times there are those who are anxious to investigate singular traditions. To the two latter classes the little monograph on 'Pope Joan,' written by Emmanuel Rhoïdis, edited with a preface by Mr. C. H. Collette, and published by Mr. Redway, will be very acceptable. The author discusses the topic with much learning and ingenuity, and Mr. Collette's introduction is full of information."—*Globe.*

GEORGE REDWAY, YORK STREET, COVENT GARDEN.

Sphinx :

Monatsschrift für die geschichtliche und experimentale Begründung der übersinnlichen Weltanschauung auf monistischer Grundlage herausgegeben von HUBBE SCHLEIDEN,

Dr. J. U.

1s. 6d. monthly ; 12s. per annum.

"We cordially recommend this magazine to all those of our readers who are acquainted with the German language, as it promises to be one of the best extant periodicals treating of transcendental subjects."—*The Theosophist.*

GEORGE REDWAY, YORK STREET, COVENT GARDEN.

Transactions of the London Lodge of the Theosophical Society:

Nos. 1 and 2.—Out of print.

No. 3.—On the Higher Aspect of Theosophic Studies. By MOHINI M. CHATTERJI.

No. 4.—A Synopsis of Baron Du Prel's "Philosophie der Mystik." By BERTRAM KEIGHTLEY.

No. 5 —A Paper on Reincarnation. By Miss ARUNDALE. And other Proceedings.

No. 6.—The Theosophical Movement. By A. P. SINNETT.

No. 7.—The Higher Self. By A. P. SINNETT.

No. 8.—The Theosophical Society and its Work. By MOHINI M. CHATTERJI.

No. 9.—A Paper on Krishna. By MOHINI M. CHATTERJI.

No. 10.—On Mesmerism. By A. P. SINNETT.

No. 11.—Theosophy in the Works of Richard Wagner. By W. ASHTON ELLIS.

Nos. 3 to 11, and each succeeding number as issued, may be had, price One Shilling.

GEORGE REDWAY, YORK STREET, COVENT GARDEN.

In the press.

MR. SWINBURNE'S NEW POEM.

A Word for the Navy.

BY

ALGERNON CHARLES SWINBURNE.

Edition limited to 250 copies, each numbered.

GEORGE REDWAY, YORK STREET, COVENT GARDEN.

A few copies only remain of the following important work, by the author of " The Rosicrucians."

Phallicism:

Its connection with the Rosicrucians and the Gnostics, and its Foundation in Buddhism.

BY

HARGRAVE JENNINGS,

AUTHOR OF "THE ROSICRUCIANS."

Demy 8vo., cloth.

"This book is written *ad clerum*, and appeals to the scholar only, and not to the multitude. It is a masterly and exhaustive account of that worship of the creative powers of nature which, under various names, has prevailed among all the nations of antiquity and of mediæval times, alike in Egypt and India, in Italy and Gaul, among the Israelites of old, and among the primitive inhabitants of Great Britain and Ireland . . . . a most valuable auxiliary to all who care to pursue such a subject of inquiry, a subject for which Mr. Jennings is the better fitted on account of his long and intimate acquaintance with the Rosicrucians, their tenets, and their practices."—*Antiquarian Magazine and Bibliographer.*

" Unpleasant as this subject is, we are quite prepared to agree that in its scientific aspect, as a form of human worship, it has considerable importance . . . . Mr. Jennings deals almost entirely with the subjective part of his inquiry, and he has evidently made a considerable amount of research into the literature of early religions. . . . . He has produced something which is, at all events, worth the attention of the student of comparative psychology."—*Antiquary.*

" This book. . . is profoundly learned, and gives evidence on each page of deep thought, intense powers of research, clear and unmistakable reasoning, and thorough mastership of the subject. The appendix also contains much very curious matter which will interest those who desire to study the subject under all its different aspects and bearings."—*Reliquary.*

GEORGE REDWAY, YORK STREET, COVENT GARDEN.

544 *pages, crown 8vo., green cloth boards, price* 7s. 6d. (*Only* 500 *copies printed.*)

Dickensiana.

A Bibliography of the Literature relating to CHARLES DICKENS and his Writings.

Compiled by FRED. G. KITTON, author of "'Phiz' (Hablôt K. Browne), a Memoir," and "John Leech, Artist and Humourist." With a Portrait of "Boz," from a Drawing by SAMUEL LAURENCE.

"This book is honestly what it pretends to be, and nothing more. It is a comprehensive catalogue of all the writings of Mr. Charles Dickens, and of a good quantity of books written about him. It also contains copious extracts from reviews of his works and from sermons on his character. The criticisms are so various, and some of them are so much at variance with others, that the reader of them can complain of nothing less than a lack of material on which to form his judgment, if he has not formed it already, on the claim of Mr. Dickens to occupy a front place in the rank of English classics. Assertions, if not arguments, are multiplied on either side."—*Saturday Review.*

"Mr. Kitton's task has obviously involved much labour and research, and it has, on the whole, been very ably performed."—*Scotsman.*

"The labour involved in the preparation of such a volume is, of course, enormous, but all Dickens students and collectors will thank Mr. Kitton for his work. The volume contains a finely-executed portrait of Dickens, from a drawing by Samuel Laurence."—*Graphic.*

"It is a very full and delightful book; for open it at any page, and you are almost certain to come upon some interesting fact or fancy, the thought of a man of genius, or an incident bearing on a memorable life and its work."—*St. James's Gazette.*

"A great deal that relates in numberless ways to the best known and most loved of English humorists will be found in this volume, certainly the most comprehensive that has yet essayed to illustrate his popularity from every personal and critical point of view."—*Daily Telegraph.*

"Mr. Fred. G. Kitton . . . . has done his work with remarkable thoroughness, and consequently with real success. It is a subject on which I may fairly claim to speak, and I may say that all I know, and a great deal I did not know, about Dickens is to be found in Mr. Kitton's work."—"Atlas," in the *World.*

"DICKENSIANA."
"If with your Dickens-lore you'd make
   Considerable headway,
The way to be well-read's to take
   This book brought out by REDWAY.
'Tis clear, exhaustive, and compact,
   Both well arranged and written;
A mine of anecdote and fact,
   Compiled by F. G. KITTON."—*Punch.*

GEORGE REDWAY, YORK STREET, COVENT GARDEN.

INDEX.

	PAGE
Astrology Theologized	32
Anatomy of Tobacco	17
Antiquarian Study	24
Astrologer's Guide	26
Archæology and Occultism	29
Adams, F. W. L.	32
Adams, Mrs. Davenport	34
Arundale, Miss	36
Baughan, Rosa	8, 14, 17
Blavatsky, H. P.	21, 26
Burma	22
Batty, John	24
Bonatus	26
Browne, Hablôt K.	30
Betts, B. W.	31
Beauty and the Beast	34
Chirognomancy	17
Cosmo de' Medici	11
Curate's Wife, The	14
Colman's Plays	19
Confessions of an English Hachish Eater	20
Cruikshank, George	25
Church, W. E.	25
Cardan	26
Cook, Miss Louisa S.	31
Collette, C. H.	35
Chatterji, Mohini M.	36
Dickens	5
Dickensiana	38
East Anglian	18
Eliphas Levi's Writings	30
Forlong, Major-General J. G. R.	12
Forty Vezirs	13
Folk-Songs	23
Geometrical Psychology	31
George, G. M.	7
Gibb, E. J. W.	13
Greville Nugent	17
Hints to Collectors	5, 6
Hubbe-Schleiden, J. U.	35
Heptameron	10
Horne, R. H.	11
Hartmann, F.	10, 16
Hermes	33
Illumination	15
Incidents in the Life of Mme. Blavatsky	26
Ingram, John H.	21
Johnson, C. P.	5, 6
Jones, Ebenezer	24
Jones, Sumner	24
Judge, W. Q.	33
Jennings, Hargrave	37
Keightley, B.	36
Kitton, F. G.	13, 30, 38
Kent, Charles	7
Kabala Denudata	27
Kingsford, Mrs. Anna, M.D.	32, 33
Lamb	34
Leech	13
Linton, W. J.	24
Lilly	26
Leolinus Siluriensis	17

	PAGE
Low Down	27
Literature of Occultism and Archæology	29
Leicester	32
Marchant, W. T.	9
Martinengo-Cesaresco, Countess	23
Mathers, S. L. M.	27
Maitland, E.	15
Machen, A.	10
Magic	10
Mountaineering below the Snowline	10
Navy	36
Nesfield, H. W.	31
Northamptonshire Notes and Queries	30
Occult World Phenomena	16
Olcott, H. S.	28
Occultism and Archæology	29
"Phiz"	30
Physiognomy	8
Primitive Symbolism	12
Palmistry	14
Panton, J. E.	14
Paracelsus	16
Pope Joan	35
Praise of Ale	9
Poe	11, 21
Paterson	10
Path, The	33
Phallicism	37
Raven, The	21
Regular Pickle, A	31
Rideal, C. F.	15
Rueing of Gudrun	18
Sphinx	35
Sultan Stork	3
Sheykh-Zada	13
Sinnett, A. P.	15, 16, 26, 36
Sweeting, W. D.	30
Spiritual Hermeneutics	32
Sea Songs and River Rhymes	34
Shepherd, R. H.	11, 19, 24, 34
Swinburne, Bibliography of	4
Sithron	11
Scott, J. G.	22
Studies of Sensation and Event	24
Serjeant, W. C. Eldon	26
Theosophy, Religion, and Occult Science	28
Tobacco Talk	8
Theosophist, The	21
Two Tramps	27
Transactions L. L. T. S.	36
Thackeray	3, 6, 25
Tamerlane	11
United	15
Valley of Sorek	7
Virgin of the World	33
Walford's Antiquarian	20
Westropp, H. M.	12
Walford, E.	20
Wellerisms	7
White, C. H. Evelyn	18
Waite, A. E.	30
Word for the Navy	36